i kNow wHy oLd mEn sIt iN frOnt
oF wiNdows aLl dAy siGhiNg
& crYing & liVing & dyIng
whEn tHe sUn goEs doWn
oN tHe ciTy aT niGht

Poems by Joseph D. Reich

Kung Fu Treachery Press
Rancho Cucamonga, CA

Copyright © Joseph D. Reich, 2020
First Edition1 3 5 7 9 10 8 6 4 2
ISBN: 978-1-950380-89-3
LCCN: 2020931906

Design, edits and layout: John T. Keehan, Jr.
Cover image: Natalia Brovchenko
Author photo: unknown
All rights reserved. No part of this publication may be reproduced or transmitted in any form or by any means, electronic or mechanical, including photocopying, recording or by info retrieval system, without prior written permission from the author.

i kNow wHy oLd mEn sIt iN frOnt
oF wiNdows aLl dAy siGhiNg
& crYing & liVing & dyIng
whEn tHe sUn goEs doWn
oN tHe ciTy aT niGht

CONTENTS

I. The Rising Fall of the Amerikan Empire

that feeling of weeping and nothing
    coming out... 1
your early morning... 2
directions on how to get through the day... 4
a character analysis of the grownup world... 6
a side of... 8
crime fighting... 9
a panoramic alley view... 11
tradition (a manual of conditions, conflicts
    & contradictions)... 15
the absolute zero... 18
nepotism... 21
the reality show host and his
    contestants i mean constituents... 22
a madman's manifesto: on tyrants
    or the life & times of tiny giants... 23
a sad dire... 31
amerika: a postmodern contemporary version... 32
the magical king dumb... 34
a different theory or relativity... 35
pardon me... 37
canned date... 39
numb... 43
can't tell you exactly what year... 45
orchard... 47
that part of the bronx... 49

how to make gefilte fish... 50
sent... 51
this is not a repeat... 52
the ridiculous spy... 53
the life of a bird on a wire... 54
ex-con... 55
homework... 57
the sketch artist man... 58
the posse... 60
land of liberty... 61

II. Will Feel Like Zero

somewhere down in the sunshine state... 65
an answer & question session... 67
like insomnia... 70
birth of rock n' roll... 71
side effects... 72
central a.c... 73
sunrise sunset and all that stuff... 76
the secret life of midge... 77
detention... 78
a blast from the past... 79
hire education... 80
sears repair... 81
days of noir... 82
how to... 84
on the state of drizzle... 86

the portrait before it became a portrait... 87
wrinkle-free phlebotomy... 92
postcard views... 97
extracurricular (activity)... 98
irregular verbs... 99
leaving port authority as a kid... 100
all those postcards been meaning to send... 102
hotel x... 117
why z?... 119
the middle ages... 120
picket fences... 122
the ole factory senses... 124
customs... 125
right around dawn... 127
the life & times of clark kent... 128
how to cut grass... 130
depression the situational kind... 132
a different form of blue... 134
the team to trust... 135
on character and reliability... 136
all the good little monsters... 137
dissecting a sheep's eye... 139
a different sort of proof... 140
american haiku... 142
the weather: munday... 144
the weather: toosday... 145
the weather: whensday... 148
the weather: thirsty... 150
the weather: frieday... 151
an ancient study of contemporary culture
    in america... 152

one of those love letters you hate to write
   during marriage . 154
brazil, brazil... 161
51 poor traits... 163
on the nature of wild turkey... 172
for t. bickle... 173
brainwash or profiles of cowardice... 176

III. Love Sonnets to a Time Forgotten

somewhere around the early seventies... 183
self-portrait (of a boy who gets his heart
   broken at a bar-mitzvah)... 186
your local tour guide... 187
warho... 189
visit from parents in the berkshires
   in the form of communication log... 190
proof of non-existence... 192
living the life... 193
what the stats don't tell you... 194
rush hour... 197
a much older young teddy roosevelt... 199
rough rider spitting up blood... 200
transference... 201
final call... 202
a postmodern version of cowboys & indians... 203
the dream... 205
the last act at the all-you-can-eat dinner theater... 207
like the hourglass figure of a miraculous
   mermaid taking off to the horizon... 209

how to make caramel apples... 210
on bernard baruch... 211
ralph & lenny... 213
rap city in blue... 214
bio-chem... 215
mosaics or how not exactly to play dominos... 217
one of those bridges never quite finished
    and knowing the spots not to step in... 218
ghetto... 219
all-inclusive... 220
a different sort of sunblock... 221

I guess all we can really hope for is a 6 pack of beer and good bowel movement

-ex boss

I.

tHe riSing fAll of tHe ameRikan emPire

that feeling of weeping and nothing coming out,

we become news junkies
because we can't stand
the bullshit going down
in our everyday reality
having been betrayed
over and over again
and in an abusive way
almost feel like this might
help to heal the damage.
we take a dysfunctional
disproportionate peculiar
amount of pride in perennials
and the trees we planted
looking forward
to the lightning
in the near distance
like a blinking antenna
way up atop the mountain
communicating with
god and its citizens
looking forward to the rain
coming down in buckets
hoping to somehow heal
just a bit the pain experiencing
like someone habitually
reading the obituaries
the bible and betting.

your early morning...

& so we wake up each & every morning
to that little white cube-shaped tv on our
kitchen counter to *good morning america*
the taper telling us about *u.s. forces killed
...church fires...college scandal...a miracle
rescue...* you wonder how your wheat
& soybeans & porkbelly are you are
& how you are going to make it & be
able to drag your tired ass & wasted
soul through all that bumpadabumpa
to make your quota while your soulless
dispatcher who's never lived it or done
it before adding 3 more clients to your
caseload, as you crawl back home at
nightfall with secondary trauma trying
(not even trying anymore) to forget it
all, wasted, bleary-eyed past that glowing
lit-up movie theater & mall along the high-
way like some too sane insane coliseum of
suburbia & you no longer are thinking
about wheat & soybeans & porkbelly
but how you are going to even be able
to get up the next morning & go through
the exact same ritual & routine of being &
how living or reality or whatever you wanna
call it all seems like neverending states of
denial for purposes of survival even feeling

strangely profoundly alone & alienated
when seeing & hearing that artificial
sprinkler system go on (but not a living
breathing soul around) of your insane slave
insurance man neighbor always aloof &
arrogant & paranoid & guarded literally
taking on the form of a real-life snake
in the grass *claiming* like some phony
unconvincing cliched commercial he does
it all for the sake of family & has screaming
sessions each & every evening because
of some dog barking & can't help but
to wonder with a sense of awe & the tree
frogs & fireflies going off what it's all for?

directions on how to get through the day,

everyone has a hole in their soul
those who claim they don't
are full of it and lying to you
and just trying to get by on
a day by day basis and might
just try to operate and function
maybe with a trip to puerto rico
y'isreal rv'ing out to yosemite or
the grand canyon a cruise to save
the marriage picking up chocolate
and flowers for their partners when
they fuck up after they feel bad and
the guilt kicks in a microscope for
the kid to see things that can't
be peeped in the real world and
all just a little bit clearer some
who claim to be these great
providers or good family men
but if get to know them as crooked
as they come who will stray with those
chocolate and flowers in their powder-blue
tuxedos feeling proud reborn young again
taking short cuts to their lovers at dusk
some who just sit in front of windows
all day real-life innocent bystanders
watching leaves fall one by one by
one by one seagulls coming in from

the ocean at sundown squawking like
mad ice storms brooks suddenly filling
up into raging rivers drug dealers hustlers
lovers meeting on the corner all for the exact
same reason the puerto rican girls in their
parochial school dresses full of passion
and spirit gathering up at the bus stop
how the change of seasons all really
one of those silent films or form of
vaudeville keystone cops and robbers.

a character analysis of the grownup world,

i remember when i used to live in brooklyn and
there was this miserable old woman who used
to always act real suspicious whose son had
overdosed on heroin and used to spend all day
hanging out like security or a real life timekeeper
(of reality) keeping an eye out on the garbage
and one day in the early morning maybe just a
bit tired or with a hangover just threw it out
regularly as she decided to real rudely start
yelling at me and was not in the mood to take
it (as have always hated people like this who
try to blame you for all their misery) while
walking away just told her to fuck off; when
i eventually moved to my next apartment i
guess sick of being watched by the garbage
patrol, i swear there was this awful morbidly
obese super who'd spend all day and night
outside my window literally sucking up his
phlegm and spitting (and doing nothing with
his existence but harass the tenants) and for the
most part obeyed the rules of separating my
garbage yet on the morning of my uncle's
funeral who had just died of aids and heading
to the subway to his partner's loft in nyc this
fuck-up with absolutely no respect or regard for
others (or had it all delusionally rationalized like
this act of throwing out your trash represented

something between good and bad and virtue
and sin) and decided to just start hollering at me
i swear at the top of his lungs (even threatened
to out me) about the rules and regulations of
perishables and recyclables and thought o my
god aren't these disgusting and pathetic images
just the perfect metaphor (so literal almost not
a metaphor at all) for the grownup world

when i finally at last decided to report him to
the landlord of course got no return phone call.

a side of,

i always hated people
who thought they were
saying such profound shit
like you only live once while
if they only knew how much
living i had already done as
it was these exact people
who always made me
take off and hit the road
and leave and seek completely
different company and options
in this absurd reality and existence
where people just talk way too much
shit and don't seem to ever fucken listen
the waitresses don't treat the busboys
very well, the cashier doesn't treat
the waitress too good, and the owner
treats them all like garbage, while try
to instantly just forget about them all
having had my blintzes and kielbasa
and seltzer with lemon and my little
slice of heaven sitting all day in the
window of *odessa's* watching all
the hustlers and madmen shuffle
by just trying to get by in this life.

crime fighting,

i had been feeling really
insecure recently down
on my luck and that just
could not trust one single
living breathing soul and
suddenly saw where on
the superhighway they
were selling those ole
time wonder woman
truth lassos bullet
proof bracelets
where you can
ricochet and
fend off any
sort of gunfire
from the general
specific idiotic
public and instead
of that tiara with
a red star on it
a kind of unisex
patriotic helmet
and now i find
myself on a
daily basis
feeling so
much more

secure shuffling
down my driveway
feeling like a brand
new man decked-out
with my truth lasso
bullet proof bracelets
red white and blue
helmet to pick up
my junk mail with
those clip-out coupons
for a lifetime of satisfaction
such as frozen orange juice
barbasol shaving cream hot
pockets and hotel bar butter
who was it mick jagger said
sometimes i just want to
wrap my coat around you.

a panoramic alley view,

I.

i think the reason
        why i've always
                been fixated
                        intoxicated
    by that one blinking star
                blaring
                    high up
                        in the brilliant

silent quiet
emptiness
                            of real-life
                    abandonment
        in my
            down & out
                deserted room

                    millions of miles
                    away from home
    is intuitively
        spiritually
            some
                how
                    strangely
            always

    felt known
  while
    straight-up
     the only thing
      that's never
       let me down

II.

that same sacred solitary star
  in the sweltering summery
    maddening magnolia
      of new orleans

  right over the silhouetted mountains
    before sunrise in north country

at the end of the *burlington northern*
   of that brokedown motel in reno

through my gleaming glistening window
   all alone at the end of the world
in tenderloin san francisco

  leaning back in wasted easy chair
     in overgrown
       hawaiian gold
    rastafarian garden
   woebegone
  pensive

lower east side nighttime
standing completely naked
    in kitchen
      contented
        with lover

    sleeping in bedroom
brooding over warm hissing radiator
through steamy window

    out to the deep snows
      blow glowing streetlamps
        in the foghorns
          of sleepy hollow
out my solitary window
  flashing right above

      the still lovely
        cobblestone
    of sacre-coeur
  monmartre

taking off bleary-eyed
  couldn't have felt more
    anonymous liberating
      or a part of things
        on the tgv
out to the palms
  & plane trees
    of nice
      hugging

                    the miraculous
            mediterannean

    hanging holy
            over ferry
                    contemplating
                            nihilistic reality
    my only beacon
            of being
                    on-the-run
                            to the misty cliffs
                                    of palermo.

tradition (a manual of conditions,
conflicts & contradictions)

you were
the one seen
at all of those
family get-togethers
stuck in the corner
mumbling to the
grandfather clock
the one most likely
to make nothing of
yourself while those
asshole schmucks
passed gossip
and rumors
passed down
from generation
to generation
that flock of
uncles who
made it
a tradition
to huddle
in circles
and tell riddles
about other religions
then gather around
the television with
their thanksgiving

fixings full of piping
hot turkey stuffing
and ambrosia to
watch all those
all-american
teams like
the redskins
vs cowboys
the one working
security bragging
about how many
people he's got
working beneath
him that arrogant
phony idiot who
would feign curiosity
and interest and ask
you questions and
right when started
answering would
automatically like
some subhuman
automaton turn
away and walk
in the other direction
while not too ironic
or by coincidence
inherited his daddy's
plastic business who
conveniently cheated

on his wife of 40 years
and just like that traded
her in for a newer and
more improved model
that evil anesthesiologist
who used to fondle you
on the sunken couches
during christmas vacation
husband i swear ironically
a salesman for *laz-y boy*
and then later on make
up cruel and inaccurate
mean-spirited accusations
to deflect her disgusting acts
as if nothing ever happened
while actually saved her
daughter in the midst of
crisis cause she was just
too afraid to come to her
and what she might do
to her but you never gave
up and kept on and persisted
and like that advertisement
for *timex 'took a licking
and kept on ticking'* just
like the heartbeat of that
grandfather clock standing
stoically in the corner
whispering one-liners
forever and ever.

the absolute zero,

i was born when life was getting the better of
me during one of those infamous infomercials
matter of fact i am that infomercial during
an episode of insomnia when having racing
thoughts & can't get shut eye after all the reruns
of sports & weather & barometer & dew point
right below the leftover droopy moon with a
30 day risk-free trial & offer & free shipping &
handling & satisfaction guaranteed easily stored
& just in case mom is getting bored can just put
me right up on the kitchen sill with some sort
of psychotic grin when she is making her famous
fried chicken or when i grow up to become that
token navy seal with one of those very manly
nicknames like tonto & of course return an
all-american hero & back to civilian life with
something like a very stern & stoic & earnest
expression & if just happen to be standing there
with the conviction or in the cruel conditions
right in the middle of the baking desert or
whipping ocean or retired & a part of one
of those horrible cookie cutter condos can
just put me conveniently on while all of this
gets reported by some poor & ridiculous
raconteur very neatly stored right next
to that before & after nightmare who's gotten
a bit of a bad rap the monster under the bed

& can take me practically anywhere just fold
me up like a brand new man (branded a brand
new man) in your suitcase when taking your
all-inclusive vacation while just standing
there with those other middle-aged mover
& shaker schmuck salesmen nursing your
margarita having very confident casual
conversation right there in the middle
of the bright blue pool or at one of those
reunions or those required annual very
responsible business trips having to meet
your quota & pay off the credit card &
mortgage & wife & kids & will instantly
guarantee antecdotes & clever quips &
will be there in crisis during thick & thin
& practically any stage of growth & develop-
ment in your mysterious mistaken identity muted
motel room when in truth life is just getting the
better of you & feeling so down in the dumps
& blue & just want to put a bullet right in
your brain so damn sick of playing the same
game same insane role of one roll pad of butter
regular glass of oj prepackaged cup of joe so
sick of all those same goddamn bosses looking
something like a cross between a pedophile &
politician having a difficult time making the
distinction between the innocent bystander &
serial killer having become immune to all the
bullshit simply going through the motions
feeling like a live wire with a deadpan sense

of humor wondering if you are just that kid
all grown up on the back of a box of cereal
hollow & hysterical never quite finding that
pot of gold at the end of the rainbow moving
from town to town like some unconvincing
actor with unconvincing lines some salesman
in disguise with his awful contrived shtick
reading straight off the salesman script
some real-life prepackaged product who
deep down inside doesn't even believe himself
literally feeling every last brittle bone in your
body creaking no longer sure if you are the
ventriloquist or dummy while perhaps maybe a
couple more banana daiquiri's might *do the trick*
realizing none of this really matters the origins
or the parroting so getting back to reality &
the baseline of everyday functioning i'm
the answer to all your problems & worries
all your pain & all your suffering with
a satisfaction guarantee of the eternal
happily ever after in only 3 easy payments.

nepotism,

i want to be in one of those tv commercials
with one of those 20 somethings with their
perfect health club bodies in their bathing
suits and bikinis always gleeful celebrating
and toasting each other by the sea (as this
is all they ever do cause of old money and
connections and daddy's little girl but my
luck i'll be put on the production crew
responsible for putting out the big deli
cold cut platter) no matter the beautiful
girls will make their own perfect little
circle for me by the sea toasting me
with their light beer bottles while
i lie back hysterical in my wicker
recliner just like fdr used to with
his long penguin cigarette holder
knowing sincerely in reality with
my satire have made the world
just a little safer for democracy.

the reality show host and his
contestants i mean constituents,

the commander-in-chief tweets–

*we're running like a smooth
well-oiled machine!*

what was that expression again
about rome burning?

oi-vey-iz-mir

yiddish translation:

every man for himself...

a madman's manifesto: on tyrants
or the life & times of tiny giants,

1.

bullet point: we now have a tyrant who has had
his token temper-tantrum & threatened with
blackmail & a real-life ultimatum, presently
holding the country hostage using the people
as pawns & puppets & possessions because
wouldn't give him his funds to build his
silly little sci-fi psychotic wall & instantly
shut down the government

2.

bullet point: we have a thief who threw his hat
in the ring & developed his reputation just
like mccarthey based on false accusations &
conspiracy & demagoguery, racist innuendo
& implications that our first black president
was not born in this country & thus did not
earn the honor & respect (the personification
of prejudice & emotional neglect) of his title
& standing

3.

bullet point: we have this higher-than-holy,
soulless hotelier who made his millions by
bilking the public off trump wine, trump air
lines, trump university & trump enterprises,
while declared bankruptcy multiple times
& still not paid back a majority of his
backers, contractors & all those *illegals*
who helped build his quasi-empire; this
real-life automaton gimmick product who
literally thrives off the bully pulpit with his
background audience of brainwashed idiots
& like some telemarketer-monster feeds off
them like godzilla attacking engulfing getting
recharged by the live electric wires of the wild
chaotic masses

4.

bullet point: we have someone clearly &
clinically with a psychological hx of being
a pathological, compulsive liar who will
change the facts of the matter & his allegiance
to however it best suits his advantage & will be
histrionic & confrontational & defensive & go
on the all out attack & *offensive* with a very
weak & fragile identity & ego & traits &

characteristics which mimic & parrot &
even overlap some of the symptoms of
borderline personality, at times multiple
personality & undoubtedly some arrested
stage of development

5.

bullet point: we have an individual who has
not mastered a number of the mature stages
of growth & development & thus presents
as fragmented & frustrated with *a fear of
intimacy* while often displays a tendency
to turn passive-aggressive, mean-spirited
& instantly hostile

6.

bullet point: we have some little rich kid
obnoxious spoiled brat who has always
been given the easy route (taken the *easy
way out*) & in periods of crisis been able
to be bailed-out (privileged & entitled) &
thus as a character analysis has a thought
pattern cognitively distorted & does in many
ways think *the world revolves around him*
(with clinical delusions of grandeur & when
he doesn't get his way, persecution) so in fact

does not have the ability to be compassionate
(sympathetic or empathetic) & with that
cognitive disconnect rarely shows any sense
of guilt or conflict or remorse so with these
clinical features can even be assessed in certain
cases of severe & profound consequence
with a potential diagnosis as sociopathic

7.

bullet point: we have some schmuck who after
the central park 5 through d.n.a. testing were
found innocent & cleared of all crimes (saw
jail time) opined that we should still give
them the death penalty

8.

bullet point: we have some freak who announced
his candidacy coming down the gold-gilded
escalator of his corrupt criminal kingdom
based on the notion that all mexicans are
gang members & rapists & drug dealers

9.

bullet point: we have some reality show
belligerent barker who tries to brainwash us
(on the deal & delusion) to keep our borders
safe & secure keeps children locked up in cages
while meeting the criteria & all the symptoms of
clinical narcissism pulls out of all necessary
agreed-upon international treaties, denies
global warming, mass shootings & has no
problem sleeping with all of these other
crude forms of genocide & atrocities

10.

bullet point: we have some ventriloquist/dummy
falsely claim with his tally of already 17,000
recorded lies growing by the day (like the national debt)
that when the world trade center went down he actually
saw crowds of palestinians dancing wildly
in the streets of jersey

11.

bullet point: we have some punk who boasted
how he could shoot someone right in the middle
of 5th avenue & would face absolutely no
consequences & get away with it

12.

bullet point: we have some prop comic with
his u.s.a. cap on & oompa-loompa makeup
tossing paper towels to hurricane victims
in puerto rico & survivors of wildfires who
have lost it all giving them advice & criticism
about prevention & how to properly sweep
the forest floor, who ridicules & mocks
his attorney general for simply doing his
job & refers to him as elmer fudd & his
democratic rival as pocahontas; a real
life caricature why called the ugly
american & white devil

13.

bullet point: we have a commander-in-chief
complete control freak who absurdly has tried
to not only keep down & manipulate all key
established forms of democracy & free speech
but even history where the stocks have dropped
& plummeted to an all-time low on christmas
eve which has not been seen since the great
depression & fired almost every member of
his cabinet leaving the cupboard empty &
abandoned like prince hamlet perseverating
wandering & pacing the floors of his castle

14.

bullet point: in conclusion when we speak about the nature & behavioral patterns of kings & tyrants isn't this exactly what we were warned about & what the revolutionary war & civil war & world war II & the declaration of independence & emancipation proclamation & constitution all represented & what we fought & died for & so when we have an ignorant stubborn leader who knows absolutely nothing about our past nor american hx (a real-life self-fulfilling prophecy & unwilling to learn or ever even admit that he's wrong) are we not bound & at high-risk for at least repeating the exact same mistakes?

15.

bullet point: so i implore you what does it finally take & how much do we have to be pushed & played (& betrayed) where is that one single sincere brave soul & man of courage & honesty & integrity who is not afraid & a slave to politics & their constituency & maybe even be like one of those real-life statesmen or forefathers from back in the day of individuality & independent thinking & willing to actually serve & sacrifice themselves for the good of the country & stand up to this see-through blatant & obvious abuse of power tyranny?

16.

bullet point: chuck d. of the infamous rap group *public enemy* prophetically politically poignantly pleaded — *if you don't stand up for something you'll fall for everything.*

a sad dire,

the commander-in-chief
announced enthusiastically
over his tweet (with plenty
of explanation points) how
they're going to increase
and place multiple tariffs
on peter pan (peanut butter)
in iran due to sudden attacks
of oil refineries in saudi arabia
over the weekend; commander
in chief, unaware, due to dx
and features and symptoms
a cognitive disconnect and
grandiose sense of self
meeting all criteria (in the
dsm) for narcissistic personality
disorder was the original cause
for this attack as iran deemed
it a declaration of war when
originally pulled out of the
nuclear accords (due to a very
insecure and fragile identity
and ego) trying in every way
shape and form to get back
at his arch-nemesis obama
and now apparently multiple
tariffs placed on peter pan
(peanut butter) in iran...

amerika: a postmodern contemporary version

after jfk got blown away and his brains flew
out all over the place and jacqueline bouvier's
animal instincts kicked in and tried to escape
to safety crawling from the back of that black
convertible (that's the part upon reflection that
actually made me weep) and the secret service
pulled her back in america became instantly
transfixed and fixated with all those conspiracy
theories as for me i've always been something
of a realist and cared more about how that mad
scientist embalmer had to piece piece by piece
his skull back together again bone and flesh and
fragments and skin to try and make him look
presentable before they placed his coffin in the
back of that air force one plane where under
a literal shroud of darkness and mystery (even
shame) lbj directly sworn into office camelot
catastrophically crumbled and jackie now
a black widow stood stoically still in shock by
his side while always wondered how she was
able to survive or function and thrive and go
back like i guess lincoln's bride to the white
house while if it was me i swear i think would
have hitch hiked halfway cross country probably
holed-down into like some *motel 6* in the middle
of the desert or one of those closed-down
abandoned off-season resorts right off the
coast of oregon when all those mad haunting
winds and rains came in then took off to sicily

when her motherly instincts told her she had to
protect her kids as her claim at the time (as well
as thought-pattern) was if they're trying to kill
kennedys i'm outta here and became something
of a runaway bride while guess just being
something of a realist don't think america's
ever truly rebounded or recovered (or mourned
properly) as just a little later on they got his
brother and then martin and malcolm or perhaps
maybe america (like everything else with the
psychodynamic of defense-mechanisms and
post-traumatic stress disorder) just went through
the motions and woke up the next day like the
walking dead disassociating like nothing ever
happened right back into bumpadabumpa traffic
having to pay off their mortgages the images of
vietnam constantly flashing across television
a man on the moon with some sci-fi capsule
coming down from outer-space (commercials
for *tang*) all those cult murders in la watergate
inflation those insane neverending gas lines and
kind of strange how it all sort of comes around
full circle and we now got this pseudo-wannabe-
prima-donna-playboy-wax-museum-reality-show
president actually far worse than anything
manufactured by richard millhouse nixon
(who ironically with traits and characteristics
of severe paranoia saw himself too as something
of a martyr and victim) runs all his businesses
and quasi-kingdoms women and present day
white house something like a real-life mafia
syndicate coming down that gold-gilded
elevator while in fact remember exactly where...

the magical king dumb,

it's of my deepest conviction most shallow
belief that after his presidency trump's going
to pass the torch onto mickey mouse with
goofy as his vp donald duck for his secretary
of state the muted and classy cinderella for
first lady and snow white and the 7 dwarfs
his privileged and entitled spoiled brat children
who through multiple marriages and multiple
women nepotism and absolutely no experience
(just a blind belief in them from all the
traits and characteristics and criteria for
diagnosis of textbook clinical narcissistic
personality disorder from the diagnostic
statistic manual) will run the world and
will invite over all the international mad
men and megalomaniacs and dictators to
his posh magical kingdom resort i kid you
not as is the next natural step in the passing
of the torch after oprah and arnold bow out
of the running and here comes mickey in his
mickey mouse ears waddling up to the podium.

a different theory of relativity,

in amerika they used to throw pizza parties
to find out who shot jr sometimes for study
groups to obtain your doctorate of course
the superbowl and maybe to get some
kind of buzz a couple wine coolers and
brews and if you were one of those rich
spoiled obnoxious brats who the rules never
applied to and faced no consequences 'cause
daddy's lawyer would always bail them out
meticulously divide up those lines of coke
and decide which one you want and snort
it right up while now we get take-out and
gather around the idiot box to find out
how many years just another corrupt
government official or campaign manager
got for years and years of a life of defrauding
the american public embezzlement nepotism
abuse of power and showing absolutely
no remorse or contrition snickering with
his lawyer in the lobby showing up to the
courtroom in his final obvious see-through
disguise decked-out in token wheelchair just
like that manipulative old man and evil prede-
cessor vice president cheney at the inauguration
with all his war crimes and atrocities trying to
elicit sympathy and of course as always claiming
to be real good fathers and family men while

the classless judge pretty much of the same class
and social strata attending the same symbolic
countryclub and college gives him a reduced
sentence as is a natural understood tradition
and custom for the male caucasian in amerika
right around the same age and feels sympathy
and of who he is really able to relate to and
make some sort of true-blue connection

thomas jefferson & benjamin franklin rolling...

pardon me,

i hear trump is handing out pardons
like some game show where you take the
money and run or try to guess what's behind
the curtain or one of those drive-thru cathedrals
where on the screen they'll tell you if you've
been absolved of your sins with a couple
token hail marys for when you get home;
also helps i guess for a little nepotism and
to be friends with kim kardashian because
of all her meetings with his son-in-law
jared (who of course plans on bringing
peace to the middle east now getting
nailed for all these crooked real estate
dealings) and all her ideas for prison reform;
just heard he pardoned this 63 year old mom
doing a lifetime bid for selling coke and hear
the next one on his list is poor martha stewart.
i'm thinking of just showing up due to all
my guilt and to confess about that girl in
brooklyn who used to be a ballerina and
lived in the apartment right above me and
heard she liked me and once brought home
made rum balls to my door and like some
moron i just stood there and didn't know
how to act and still regret and feel remorse
for my lack of action. it's shit like that that
always haunts me and have a history of being

way too tough on myself yet thinking of just
showing up to 1600 pennsylvania avenue
(mockingbird lane) if in fact they're giving
out pardons as might help to relieve just
a bit of my guilty conscious.

canned date,

1

i have decided the next best most viable
candidate will be that infamous black box as
when it all comes down to it doesn't talk back
and i guess the only thing in real life that truly
has our back the only thing that can sincerely
be believed and relied on and honestly report
and record all of life's hardships and difficulties
and hypocrisies and contradictions; all its true-
blue course of events and truths and falsehoods;
only thing empirically earnestly keeps its word

2

get rid of all the fluff and peanut butter on
wonder get rid of the metaphorical 'man behind
the curtain' get rid of the dummy-ventriloquist
act and get real results as opposed to all those
false promises and bullshit and betrayal and
will just input all our problems and conflicts
and issues and social and cultural dilemmas
into the core soul of its speakers just sitting
there all square and bare without all that
smoke and mirrors right on the table

3

i was thinking when all those really annoying
harassing useless companies get back to me
over the superhighway and always want me
to take one of their inane surveys (everything
in amerika these days based on some sort
of approval rating) just finally respond like
some maniacal mechanical machine blowing
its top (as some kind of sarcastic payback)
which will be so damn cathartic of *dead
n/a not available*

4

when i die i just want to light myself on fire
into one of those eternal, everlasting, reliable
yule logs and when they all finally find out
i was a man of integrity and honor simply
pull the plug

5

somewhere around the mid-seventies where they
had that cultural phenomenon of a gimmicky
transitional-object in all those bachelor pads in
uptown manhattan when the divorce rate just
started to skyrocket of just flicking a switch
on the wall and there'd be this instant automatic
romantic mock fire and think there's something

really to be said about that
with a stash of the single's mom marijuana
neatly and conveniently wrapped in a sand
wish bag in the drawer of the night table

6

the ventriloquist's dummy leaves his teeth
with the old lady at the welfare hotel
and now just has no tale to tell
which is really the most telling
like kids playing pin the tail
on the donkey blindfolded
disoriented staggering
over to jesus on a
model glue crucifix

7

i think if there was a real-life reenactment
of jesus' last supper the exact same things
and lies and betrayals and plotline and fable
(due to the horrible futile pattern of human
behavior and nature) would just happen
over and over and over again...

8

i'm holy recommending
a black box for our
next president.

numb,

1. they should replace the national
anthem with kurt cobaine's *tourette's*

2. jesus made all the statues in the park confess

3. i could never stand those who'd make such
stoical cliche sweeping generalizations like
those who commit suicide are selfish and
cowardly or not thinking of what it might
do to their family, as it was these exact people
who might actually in fact ironically inspire me

4. it's a strange perverse psychological
phenomenon how the two-faced liar
always makes you hate yourself

5. suburbia has a tendency to exhibit similar-like
traits & characteristics & self-loathing & fixating

6. what's the purpose of the punchline
while all comes from a long-winded
riddle sadistic & mean-spirited

7. everything these days makes me anxious
& nauseous tests my central nervous system

8. culture is criminal...

9. it's all political & so much more
meaning in the sunflowers along the train
tracks racing towards uncertain destinies

10. there's certainty in the whimsical seasons

11. all those devoted father figures look drained
& violated compulsive liars with their
prepackaged proclamations

12. the swans are paranoid & defensive
looking streetwise over their shoulder

13. while the pot of gold at the end of the rain
bow is the multi-color post-apocalyptic
sun falling down at dusk over the park
never ever really getting home

14. all the windows in the kingdom are shattered

15. and in the end you're looking to meet
the stranger you think you pathetically
have fallen in love with & will save you

16. nursing a rum & coke staring out the local
bleary-eyed & broken at the poverty-stricken
projects to safe & secure shangrila where they
keep the secrets & recycle.

can't tell you exactly what year,

that whole summer some
where around 1977 was
drinking a whole heck
of a lot of *schlitz* beer
with a handsome tan
bronx runs to pick up
hawaiian gold rolling
them into thick stupid
blunts hanging out at
friends countryclubs
having wonderful
delusional dreams of
a decent future reading
sherwood anderson's
winesburg, ohio
dostoevsky's–
*the idiot, notes
from underground*
& freud's early case
studies on hysteria
listening to a whole
heck of a lot of neil
young that spiritual
american indian
twanging lead
guitar solo
the a-side

everything
you knew
& b-side
you never
listened to
i guess the
unknown future
with the early rise
& fall of the clash
falling in love with
a whole mess of girls
& think a couple may
have loved me back
never quite making
that move making
it all that more
romantic...

orchard,

yeah true i do love the concept & process
                              of mummification
   & what the ancient egyptians
            did to their pharaohs
                     for the sake of the after-
                                        world
     but i come from a culture
        of annoying overbearing yentas
              from the other side of the tracks
where they instantly embalm you
                     & stuff you & prop you
        up to look exactly like
that old entertainer
        playing piano forever & ever
              nodding-out to the neon heavens
     placed right in the dusty window
on orchard
                  where all my ancestors
                      shuffled by
              from *shapiro's wine*
   & those steamy delis & diners
on delancey
      with their guts
           full of bagels & blintzes
                         brooding

> looking
> forward
> to a future
> that might be just a slight bit better.

that part of the bronx,

the big sky state
should not be montana
but the northern bronx
when you're taking strolls
at lunch around the reservoir
during your internship at the
kingsbridge rehabilitation center
for wurzweiler school of social work
engaged having fallen in love with this
cute jewish girl to die for who still lives
with her mom in van cortland park right
on the border of yonkers and a whole
life to look forward to nothing to lose.

how to make gefilte fish,

1.pull strange fish from jar been
stewing in refrigerator for days

2. pour a very large cup of seltzer
to wash it all down with

3. watch another losing season
of the ny metropolitans

sent,

they should make a housespray
that smells exactly like those fresh
warm bagels coming directly out the brick
oven when you pick up a dozen streaming
over the cobblestone at dawn and the last
of the sputtering gleaming stars hang over
the glowing river of the meat market after
you worked a graveyard driving a cab all
night in the madness of manhattan and
literally stagger home with those fresh
warm bagels newly printed paper with
the scores from the night before and
a tall can of beer somewhere at the
end of the world where they keep
those asphalt brooding basketball
courts placid drying-out in an oasis
of puddles like the remnants of clothes
on a line in the western most part of the
west village cause you are not a criminal
like they conveniently like to portray you
as have paid your dues far more than all
of those fools put together and pass out
empty and vacant when all you hear is
the last of the holy weary echoing of the
distant stray trail of foghorns on the hudson.

this is not a repeat,

after a repeat night of insomnia
i find myself watching a repeat
of one of those late-night ball
games seeing this coach on
the sidelines having one of
his token temper-tantrums
and read his lips mutely
hollering–*lies!* and
can't help but to find
myself instantly chiming
in and sympathizing
giggling to myself–
ain't that the truth.

the ridiculous spy,

one lives something of a long, lonely, solitary,
ridiculous existence but all those reference points
and dreams which eventually always come back
to haunt him, one almost wonders and ponders
within the machinations and infrastructure of
dreams what if all those wild maddening life
experiences or references (made up of surreal
images and archetypal and psychological
symbols) never happened or were visited,
as back then were completely instinctive
(adventuresome) and perhaps had more
resilience, and an emotional and spiritual
immune system like geometrically,
metaphysically, philosophically
asking why they won't let you
alone and who needs it? it was
so much better really being just
a natural and lonesome traveler
and the leading character in a play
you were never ever really a part of.

the life of a bird on a wire,

i used to know this really wealthy philipino girl
who would tell me such stuff like how rice was
a main staple to their everyday diet even was
something *spiritual* and symbolic and within the
next week was divorcing one of my best friends
from the lebanese section of detroit, michigan
leaving him hanging and giving him something
of an existential ultimatum. i wonder if in her
rationale and reasoning ever even considered
this 'spiritual' and psychological deprivation
or did it even cross her mind? i now know why
in the opening scene of *last tango in paris*
brando was just found howling under the
el being drowned out by the rattle of the
metro and all those little things in life
that'll eventually kill you.

ex-con,

i don't know...
maybe i'm being
something of a
realist or one of
those linguists
but one of those
husbands who
ain't getting it
deprived of
the basic
necessities
like love and
sex and intimacy
and affection and
all of a sudden comes
along one of those
gorgeous little
temptresses
when he's
minding his
own business
not sure if i would
necessarily call
that cheating cause
isn't he the one who
was cheated or feels
cheated asking what

did i do to deserve this
as seems more like one
of those prisoners just
come out the pen after
having served a 3-5 bid.

homework,

after one of those long brutal days bickering
what they sometimes like to do for a living
you thinking what kind of living is this
you watch the sun go down over the hills
like one of those giant redhots you used
to chew as a kid picked up after one of
those long journeys down that sweltering
summer road to the general store. you
imagine more so looking

out your window drawing a big yellow sun
with rays coming out of it in the corner of
the sky like you used to very neatly and
organized in elementary school on that
off-white composition paper while on
the thin blue lines *today will be sunny*
and your name...april 1970

somehow at the end of the day you still manage
to feel guilty even though she was so irrational
impossible and maddening looking so cute
and fine in those shiny white strapped heels
and purple sundress with a light black sweater
tossed over the shoulders and think of that sun
you drew in 1970.

the sketch artist man,

i have always been fascinated
             with the work of sketch artists
                       having the ability
    to capture the mood of the moment
             of those sketchy individuals
                         & felt like were able
    to totally encapsulate
         their expressions & body language
                                & even
their essence
which just felt so much keener
         than their actual character
                   (or lack there of)
             & sometimes like to imagine
                  them when they're
             at home
     & their wife
         is just being some kind of nudge or nag
                                or just
driving them up the wall
         & whip out their charcoal
                   & don't really engage
                        or get involved
     when their spoiled daughter
         is making outlandish demands
                  claiming how much she

                        can't stand living there
            or those evil hypocritical neighbors
never close to the image or concept
of being neighborly

then just slips into the shower
to try & forget it all & sing a
round of the blues maybe
even an acoustic version
of good ol' bob marley
barry manilow *i'm ready*
to take the chance again!

        & rejuvenated enters the kitchen
                where instead of his kid's artwork
                        all over the refrigerator

                sketches of his wife
                        being a nudge

        his daughter being
a drama queen

        & that neighbor never once
            being close to being neighborly
                just a phony snake in the grass

                    cut-throat creep
                            making his quota
        of stretching the truth
from the shallows of the deep.

the posse,

i see the hx of culture & civilization
as simply a cross
between obsessively shining a bowling ball
& shining your shoes for the ball.
whether you have that proverbial
quote on quote ball is of course
always open to interpretation & debate
which is left till later for the wife & husband
to engage in half-crazed battle
at the bewitching hour.
when man used to round-up that infamous
posse& go galloping out of town
like gangbusters it wasn't really so much
cause he cared to catch the criminal but
in fact a form of acting-out & overcompensation
& male-bonding cuz the wife was driving him
crazy while sometimes if he got lucky
would even cross borders & boundaries.
there was a reason why billy the kid & dillinger
& bonnie & clyde rose to such great heights.

land of liberty,

a strange secret time
when they had those real-life
intellectually-inspired mad scientists
in radioactive goggles setting
off test mushroom clouds just
couple miles away from where
those tipsy martini-drinking cut
throat civil engineer insurance men
were pulling handles not just getting
their dose of healthy leisure class
tinfoil reflecting sun vizier tans
but also were scammed
& not let in on the grand plan
as future leukemia victims
of course never informed
by the c.i.a. central invest
gating guilt by association
(while the higher-ups in
advertising single-minded
neat neck ties more
obsessed with just competitively
keeping the complete illusion
alive with convenient
propaganda & brainwash
& fine one-liner jingles
of how we are the best)
& technicolor to die
for madonna-whore wives
pushing their supermarket
carts in placating stimulating

                        muzak air-conditioned utopian
                amerikan dream food emporiums
        called such things like
                piggly-wiggly with lovely
                        sweet psychotic smiles
                                        on the all-out lookout
                        for fluff & peanut butter
                & wonder bread for their first born
juvenile delinquent angels
                who will play cops & robbers
                                & cowboys & indians
                                        looking to make
                        the world safe for democracy
                in brand-new spanking suburbs
        sprouting from the hills
of the sierra-nevada's
                & real-life fire drills
                        where bright-eyed children
                                        are told to run
                        for their lives & hide
                right under desks
        & not to come out
(red rover! red rover!)
                till the threat from that
                        dangerous communist
                                mother russia is over.

II.

wIlL feEL liKe zeRo

somewhere down in the sunshine state,

you are freezing by the wood burning stove
with another foot of snow out here in vermont.
the nurse came over again to bandage up my
leg and the arthritis and edema been driving
me crazy. what else can i do but turn on the
grapefruit league where the mets are competing
against the astros somewhere down in the
paradise of port st. lucie (this is the time of
the season i love the most as those teams which
really stink and suck still think they have a
fighting chance and are all optimistic and
hopeful and make such outlandish claims
like–*if we are able to stay healthy think
we can make a good run at it* but just like
the wise ass delinquent at the beginning of
the school year who declares–*i'm going
to turn over a new leaf* and just a couple
months is heard and seen cracking one-liners
and in his natural habitat of detention). i keep
the volume off as helps to relieve a bit the
tension and notice there is no one in the stands
just the way i like it except for a few retirees
and their unhappy wives all lined up in a row
who seem miserable as always as have decided
to stick it out and stay together and seems like
even if someone hit a homer or one of those ol'
time streakers showed up in hightop sneakers

would not change at all their demeanor or body
language. i notice there is not even a single
vendor selling beer or frankfurters at the stadium
or perhaps just on a buddhist-existential level
has something of a drinking and eating disorder
or more accurately some kind of situational
depression and decided not to come out and
stay in the shadows. there is a whole line of
palms all around the outfield and not a single
one swaying in the semi-tropical heat almost
seeming like some strange sluggish stage
of evolution with crocs and stripmalls and
billboards advertising something for jai-ali
or some kind of hot dog. maybe it's just some
time around the earlybird special which caused
them to become reflective and resentful or has
just become some sort of trigger for supper
while representing something from their
childhood and how their whole life has passed
them by. it is going to end in a tie and be one
of those where the managers are going to end
up calling it and think ain't that just a lot of
what this life is all about as the channel naturally
heads out to the cactus league somewhere in
the desert with the reds taking on seattle.

an answer & question session,

1

i been thinking with all this recent
global warming shit that eventually
chunks of the coast are just going
to split off all except for some mad
zombie old timer intense and focused
right in front of his slot machine pulling
a handle in atlantic city and floating off
without even being aware of it as that's
about all we can say about the human race

2

recently i been so frustrated and steaming
with just the flakiness and poor character
of man been doing exercises like they
teach the boys in group homes when
they can't control their anger to count
backwards from ten and just decide
to erase all the saved messages on
my answering machine and realize
they're all just talking shit and saying
nothing and just love to hear the sound
of their own voices and just dream
some old long lost friend from child
hood decides to just call and leave me
a message to simply ask how i am doing

3

think i can finally relate and make
a connection to perhaps maybe those
old ancient biblical caravaggio paintings
or even michalangelos where those cherubs
& gods & rubenesque women poverty-stricken
all hunched and huddled together in loin cloths
are desperately helplessly looking up for
some sort of sign or spirit or savior

4

i heard just recently google and bill gates
are going to invest some of their fortune in
some sort of meatless burger which supposedly
oozes out a similar like liquid for those who
want to have the same experience of eating
a whopper

6

our commander-in-chief most likely has decided
to physically shut down our whole border to
mexico and continue to provide no funding
and put down puerto rico cause simply does
not like the way he's being treated

7

10, 9, 8, 7, 6, 5, 4, 3, 2, 1
blast off! the opposite
of having an explosion
or what they teach you
in the boys group home.

like insomnia,

up late at night i find myself
guzzling cold milk dreaming
the inside of the refrigerator
reads *honky-tonk* seeing a
young cary grant dressed
like a gangster on-the-run
in one of his early ones no
not that one and someone
looking like leo gorcey
holding open the door
to the getaway car still
getting paid peanuts
while later on some
mad scientist rocking
back and forth down
in his basement with
the only thing he truly
loves in this existence
after life gets the better
of him which is that robot
he is trying so passionately
to fix and to build as the perfect
companion and can't give up on
does not give that type of love
to the lovely wife who stands
nobly by his side in a bathrobe
old women trudging uphill in frisco
in those pouffy quilt dresses looking
right around the turn of the century.

birth of rock n' roll,

turtle sticks his skull out the shell
during that stage of evolution hearing
dylan's–*please crawl out your window*
like that toddler literally bopping in stroller
in washington square park listening to the
rhythm of rage against the machine…say
they respond so positively to stimulating
self-soothing of a mother's rocking cuz
that was their range of motion in utero.

side effects,

the last couple of days my phone and iced coffee
have been following me from room to room
around my home but still no calls and no sense
of being reborn; o well, what 'ya gonna do?
never asked to be born and have learned to live
alone. they say they think we're gonna get hit by
another big one before the season's over and first
time i recall in so damn long i wish it would just
all finally end and could live happily ever after,
like some guido on the boardwalk with his shirt
off and a boom box on shoulder listening to
shostakovitch and perkofiev.

central a.c.,

florida what a strange
        absurd destination
                when on winter vacation
      used to go down to visit
& in the instant
    that mad blessed humid
            semi-tropical
                heat would smack you
        right in the kisser
when you exited
            those whooshing doors
                of the airport
& the whole goal
      was just to try
            to get from the front door
                  of the condo
              (caked in *coppertone*)
        to their car
   & the shangrila
air-conditioner
      with one of those gimmicky
            mechanical voices
                which would
  pleasantly tell you
please fasten your seat belt
         & those old timers
      in tennis sneakers

  teaching you card tricks
around the pool
    & like drooling
      pavlov dogs
        trying to score
   with their grand
  daughters

who you
   just barely knew
     but felt obligated
      to from those
       suburban schools

up north
 & never really
   got it
    but the efforts
     were so romantic & noble

& return like some
   bronzed handsome
     casanova
      to the surreal
       crazy chaos

  & horrible hustle & bustle
    of jfk or laguardia

  to those filthy piles of slush
      & the stress
        & pressure
  of higher education
     which they referred

to as *very competitive*
    & would always through
       some sort of
        self-

fulfilling prophecy
  self-destructive behavior

      testing fate
    & testing the limits

  not quite meeting
     expectations

find yourself
    snickering
     hysterical
     desperate
       in detention.

sunrise sunset and all that stuff,

why whenever i get a piece accepted from like
some editor let's say like somewhere out in the
midwest he always feels the need to tell me such
things like how in his childhood in kentucky he
played some yiddish character from a production
they put on of *fiddler on the roof* i think for the
most part coming from a pretty good and decent
place trying to make a connection i suppose
having discovered i was jewish (myself
never really so much so) spending most
of my formative years being a wise ass and
acting-out and in detention hall getting mixed
messages at home and confused by all the
hypocrisies and contradictions of authority
and *tradition* dreaming out the window
not so much so about some fiddler but more
so falling asleep at night to the who's *hooligans.*

the secret life of midge,

looking back at my school days when i earnestly
applied myself turned out i was damn good at
algebra and geometry and trigonometry but
honestly can't remember a damn thing and
forgot which one is which but i can assure
you if i once scored with one of those
girls i had a secret crush on would
remember every last single part
of them from top to bottom
and be the answer to all
my problems (which got
proven much later) with
no need for logic or even
for that matter a specific
solution in fact the true
blue absolute zero and
blissful remainder with no
need to know any of the equation
instantly solving all conflicts and crises
her real life name was millicent and not midge
and had absolutely nothing to do with widgets
but a boy's natural growth and development
and tangential transcendent soul and spirit.

detention,

to me it was always the troublemakers who were
full of life and spirit—yes, perhaps maybe a bit
out there with displaced passion or hostility, so
says the know-it-all psychiatrists (like really
bad undercover agents) so much more than
those kiss asses who just played those see-
through roles and full of it, and honestly
were the real phonies and cheaters.

a blast from the past,

i can only imagine how all the brothers and
puerto ricans felt at the end of the seventies
when a bunch of white boys out there on
komiski field in chicago decided to have
some sort of sacrificial ceremony and just
m-80 and blow up all those vinyl records
with banners which read *disco sucks*
while we all know in america what that
really represents as if almost asking what
in the hell did we do to deserve this as me
personally being a white boy loved those
days k.c. & the sunshine band donna
summer and barbra streisand gloria
gayner *i will survive* spending your
whole childhood limboing lower now
below some bar at bar-mitzvahs to
prove your manhood or trying to get
her or something even more absurd.

hire education,

college surviving off dutch-apple *pop tarts*
& 6's of *coors* beer listening to the brilliant
revelation grateful dead *eyes of the world*
only thing which made me get up get down
in the maddening warmth of new orleans
staggering bleary-eyed down the hall
in just my towel & leftover cardboard
6 pack of *gee your hair smells terrific!*
shampoo & *irish spring* soap never showing
up to class & reading philosophy off other
kids' syllabi while self-educating myself

they were big on fraternities down there
and i read *nat turner's slave revolt...*

sears repair,

i find myself these days
after my nightmares just
standing there in front of
the light of the refrigerator

with nothing to do and nowhere to go.
the directions in there read what to do
in case you need to change the filter and
believe mine is way overdue and wonder

if i can just call
the sears repairman
to fix my damaged soul.

i was raised by a captain in the navy
who used to say *big boys don't cry*
and been holding it in my whole
life and now find myself crying
practically every night.

heard last sears
closed down
the other day.

days of noir,

      it's always
      just the
      little
      tiny
leftover things art
facts & tchotchkes
crumbs in midnight
      kitchen
      secret
      scribbling
      painting
      toenails
      plum
      wine
      while
      sitting up
      atop bath
      room sink
      in panties
      that makes
      you fall in
      love with
      them and
      miss them
      so terribly
      strangely
      even feel
      guilty like

clothes
tossed
hap-
haz-
ardly
halfway
hanging
dripping
delicately
right off
the lone
son sill
wedded
scarecrow
skeleton
of jesus.

how to,

in the deep sweltering
            summer morning
                        i hear my wife waking
blowing her nose
            doing her rounds
                        fast-forward
                                    back & forth
    like some cute little wind-up doll
                                in the hall
                    raised right
                            raised wrong
                                    by an overbearing
                                            impossible-to-please
abusive mom

        taking the laundry to our room
                    hitting the bathroom
                                with pine soul
                                or some other sort
of deodorizer
which supposedly
smells like bali or fresh linen

                            due to both me & my son's
                            poor grooming habits

      & then heading to the kitchen
                      for more chores

while for some strange reason
i feel just one bullet away from
blowing my brains out all over the floor.

on the state of drizzle,

through my blinds i see them transporting
the horses, refrigerators, crushed cars
like accordions, long lincoln logs,
whole mobile homes, and
always seem to be in a rush
to go nowhere not seeing a
single thing around them and
i think what kind of life is this?
when i used to deliver psycho
tropic medication & morphine
through the midnight
mountains of vermont
i always made sure
to make sure to see
everything around me
especially the young
gorgeous red hair nurses
to die for always with a killer
smile and a whole future ahead
of them and now find myself perfectly
contented nursing my *chock full o' nuts*
coffee and melancholia my mother-in-law
sent me in a care package from the bronx.

the portrait before it became a portrait.

alls i need a pair of old man pajamas
alls i need a pair of worn tennis sneakers
which smell like the beach the swamp
the cornfield and universe
alls i need a pair of windmills
when brooding about the past
and dreaming of the future
alls i need a pair of new fable & folklore
alls i need a pair of cocks & chandeliers
when i need to barter and trade it all in sick
of living the life a life of crime and playing
the real-life role of a starving artist
alls i need a pair of hostage crises hostels
hotels halfway houses in multiple languages
alls i need a pair of pancakes in bed
alls i need a pair of girls instead
one to kiss me goodnight and one
to kiss me good morning to show
me how much they really care
alls i need a pair of ladies one very large
and one very thin who will take care of me
and keep me happy through *thick and thin*
alls i need a pair of aupair girls of good bedside manner
with a bottle of pre-cum romantic vaginal discharge
alls i need a pair of strangers good-hearted
and gracious to keep me out of danger
alls i need a pair of dueling violins

preferably mozart and his vivaldi twin
alls i need a pair of nightbirds at my window
a pair of tree frogs in the pond and pair of
amphibians in the lagoon crooning
their soliloquies and blues getting
my out-of-order scar tissue heart
& soul moving again
alls i need a pair of x-ray spy glasses
i purchased in the back of those *marvel*
comics as a kid to see through the blinds
of the carnage of the freakshow carnival
in the sacrifice and slaughter at the coliseum with
that barker reality show commander-in-chief and
brainwashed staff all on their knees
alls i need a pair of pain and pleasure composed
of cheeseburger and fries and coca-cola right by
miniature golf a watchtower and insane asylum
when the sun goes down dreaming of first love
alls i need a pair of candles razorblades
notepaper and a phone number to rely on
alls i need a pair of grandfather clocks
one ticking and one not
alls i need a pair of shots moonshine
followed by hot chocolate
alls i need a pair of dice coloring
books opium loaf of rye and rice
alls i need s pair of novels buddhist
bible diagnostic statistic manual
alls i need a pair of cats and dogs
or what they call domestic animals

when my life seems foreign and lost
alls i need a pair of ghosts when
i'm at my most down and out
and helps to remind me what
i'm really about and to never give up
alls i need a pair of real-life rag dolls
one in the filthy pretty alley which
leads to the porcelain sea to keep me company
in the big bad city and one in the pristine sill
of a quaint cottage in the mirage of the country
alls i need a pair of sandwiches and drink neatly
packed in a brown paper lunch bag when i'm on
the brink with *oscar mayer* boloney moon pie
and haiku fortune cookie which keeps it all
in perspective and grounded in reality
alls i need a pair of memories which
will never give up on me
alls i need a pair of halos and battery-operated
crown of thorns one for home and one for the
road when the devils and thieves and criminals
try to steal your soul your hammer and nails
alls i need a pair of acquaintances providing
unconditional guidance and support when this
life just gets the better of you which may include
not only rivals and enemies but also friends
and family who have the uncanny ability
to quixotically underestimate misinterpret
and criminalize me
alls i need a pair of attorneys of kindness and
compassion who will sincerely go out of their

way to change the narrative and have absolutely
no idea how much more holy and sacred
so much more life experience and courage
of conviction willingness sacrifice and loyalty
than all them put together
alls i need a pair of muses when i'm at my
most con-fus-ed and the jealous devils
just being petty and trivial
alls i need a pair of shadows like late-noon
companions when i'm at my most delicate
and fragile and doubt myself
alls i need a pair of smoking smokestacks
to remind me of the real-life sediment
and ash of where i'm at
alls i need a pair of smoking chimneys
to remind me of the core of folklore
of the intimacy of beauty
alls i need a pair of strange smoking ladies
to remind me not to forget the act of forgetting
alls i need a pair of aces to double down on
somewhere between chance and consequence
and circumstance and fate in this strange
tragic theater of the absurd play half-
crazed state of grace
alls i need a pair of stairs one in the front
and one in the rear where most of life
and things and seasons begin and end
alls i need a pair of stars which resemble
a drunken slapstick comedian asleep on
the train or a connect-the-dot jesus suffering

for the sins of man who just straight up don't
seem to give a damn as saw all this illuminated
outside my solitary lonesome window of new
orleans and coney island and knew this would
somehow eternally stay with me forever
alls i need a pair of mountains when returning
home from the wreckage of the madness
of what life does to you
alls i need a pair of fresh clean dreams
to help me to finally forget my constant
stream of nightmares
alls i need a pair of duel realities to
help to remind me how trivial and petty futile and
nihilistic life really is and gets me through
it when i feel like i just can't make it.

wrinkle-free phlebotomy,

I.

i get so sick
of in amerika
all these so-called
hurricane experts
i mean seems every
one's gotta be some
sort of expert of sorts
with their very uniform
uniform in their blue short
sleeve shirts and khakis
and health club bodies
all a part of the same
happy weather team
standing very neat
and responsibly
by the shore
fuck em!
to hell
with em!
give me
the ho's!
the ho's!
the ho's!
the pimps
& prostitutes

& drag queens
clutching onto
street poles
holding on
for dear life
with wild winds
really whipping
saying such
shit like–*this*
is brown sugar
signing off
wheeeee!
and then
i can really
make my
decision
whether to
stay or to
leave

II.

streetwalker flashing
old timers in secret
alleys real-life trick
up the sleeve is the
sad story high holy
history melancholy
manifest destiny

and season of
a once thriving
crumbling town
up & coming city

III.

when i feel real lonely
i imagine purple trains
zooming through
the wintry woods
of my home never
stopping or slowing
down and delivering
phantoms to their
long-lost destiny

IV.

the lady in the cake
& how she spends
the rest of her days

V.

i view life like some ridiculous blind date
where by mistake you end up meeting
the wrong mate and end up becoming

real-life mistaken identities
which decides your fate
having nothing
to do with any
of these things
in the first place

VI.

during really rough and trying times i finally had
one of those fine redemptive dreams where bill
burroughs was just smiling telling me how much
he dug and really liked my writing to keep going
at it as i naturally humbly responded i liked his
too and to continue as well where he just grinned
and disappeared down the hall. these days what
they refer to as classical masterpieces is spider
man on dvd, as the youth walk through the towns
and cities of amerika with their heads down on
their smartphones pushing buttons, and when
they actually get on them pretend to be all
self-important like it's some honor to be around
them (having absolutely no idea what's going
on around them) i only go as far back as *atari*
and even then didn't give a damn about such
things, while was busy practicing my moves
after school and developed my reputation in
detention, and can still feel every element in
the change of seasons and the keen aroma
and hear the rhythm of the rivers and
brooks rambling through the village

VII.

i sincerely feel close to all those corny
commercials for used car lots from where
i'm from up in the high up mountains of
vermont and how in a strange psychotic
way really feel a part of the community
and environment (whatever the heck that means)
even though i know i really can't afford it and
always seems to be on that infamous miracle
mile which i ironically feel alienated and so
far from reality. i wonder what it would feel
like to be happy again? now that would be
a miracle something worth writing home

VIII.

make a killing in pork
belly and still so alone.

postcard views,

when they finally catch up to me
                    i hope they get me
                                  while i am
              very thoughtfully
gingerly picking-out
          fresh warm bagels
                  from the bin
                          at the *price chopper*

    (one of the few pleasures in life)

watching all those
          pumpernickel & poppies
                  & asiagos & everything
go tumbling down the aisle
& after those cowards tackle me
              spread-eagle
                  having already gotten
immune & used to it
from my childhood

              casually inquire
                  if they don't mind
                      if i might just be able
                            to pick
     up a package
of nova?

extracurricular (activity),

we were always these delinquent troublemakers
shoplifters who got their start at very early ages
but somehow was always able to charm
the parents especially the divorced ones
who always felt a bit more sympathetic
the vice principles proctors in detention
the teachers who always seemed to say
the same things on our report card how
he's so smart and has such great potential
but always with the need to be the class clown
and looking back even felt a little bit an honor
sometimes even for sunday school which
you were required to to become a man
to get a bar-mitzvah ironically with
the same sunday school teachers
just ten years later you were having
affairs and leading double lives in the
middle of divorces from their husbands
heading in the opposite direction on sunday
down the highway from the george washingron.

irregular verbs,

-hello, is this suicide hotline?

-no, you got cheap-o air

-o, i'd like to fly...

-where'd you like to fly?

-obviously somewhere

-roundtrip or one way?

-one way to monmartre as always

-charles degaulle?

- couldn't live up to her domestic quarrels

-i hear you...

-hey, is this suicide or cheap-o?

-cheap-o like i told you...

-if could just add couple packets of duck sauce...

leaving port authority as a kid,

always first thing in the morning
always misty (melancholy)
always steam from beneath
always those filthy streets
    appearing clean & empty
always those filthy streets
    being swept clean by sweeping machine
always shooting out that oozing disinfectant
    stream of bubbly liquid artificial clorox
    formaldehyde to keep down disease
    keep illusion alive
always those streets with real-life ghosts
    & phantoms you've already jousted
    & danced with over time
always a strange opaque transcendent
    spirit abounding
always leaving something abandoned
    once with a fine sense of belonging & now
    just distant & aloof aimlessly wandering
always those shapes & forms & delineations
    & borders which separate the city from
    bridges & rivers
always feeling taken advantage of & cheated
always feeling lied to & manipulated
always starving
always tired & weary
always bleary-eyed

always just behind & ahead of the times
always that deep pit in stomach of empty-
    nothing-void
always just above in trachea the sensation
    & need to scream & cry-out simultaneously
always on-the-run
always nothing to look back on
always something to look forward
    to something like the great unknown
always underestimated & misunderstood
    by family & the idiots of authority & society
always in perfect fighting shape to stay ready
always keen & perceptive ready for anything
always keeping eyes wide open then shutting
    warily & gently
always bus screaming mutely & leaving
    the station clandestinely triggering past surreal
    sentimental maddening adventures & realities.

all those postcards been meaning to send,

i am a steeple
i am a seesaw
i am a stonewall
i am a synagogue
i am a seesaw
& steeple
& synagogue
in the shadows
of the shutters
of a fluttering
pigeon of
a prisonyard
i am hell's kitchen
i am the lower east side
i am silicone valley
i am manifest destiny
i am washington d.c.
like a silly sibling rivalry
i am a bus escaping
from port authority
finally making it
to the city of
brotherly love
like the lost
handkerchief
of a bum
at last

like a dove
in those little
lovely coalmining
towns of pennsylvania
i am that wild spirit
meeting up with those
wandering spirits which
feel like they literally
never left the confederate
battlefields now taking
on the sacred form
of some dirty blonde
boy with a duffel bag
slung over his shoulder
somewhere on the border
right below mason-dixon
i am wilbur
& orville
with their
rickety wings
taking off from
kill devil hills
with just their
will & conviction
in the off-season
i am memphis
mobile, alabama
mississippi
in the whee
hours of the

night which
all look like
the exact same
blinking light
i am the bible
belt sighing
i am the
carolinas
crying
i am all
that magnolia
& crepe-myrtle
which can't keep
from creeping
crawling into
the chinks
& crevices
turning everything
pungent & piping
sentimental & sweet
seeping into the
haunted & holy
consciousness of
my eternal being
i am louisiana
constantly weeping
with the meek seraphim
taking off from its mausoleums
cuz sick of its incestuous history
i am chicago wailing!

i am cheyenne!
i am wy-oming!
i am the mississippi!
the mississippi!
the mississippi!
the mississippi!
flowing from slave
territory all the way
to the freedom
of stray dogs
scavenging
the slums of
detroit, michigan
i am everything
which has never
been everything
you have never
seen & will
never be
again
without
& within
i am the
madman's
mansion
i am the mad
woman whose
man keeps
on walking
out on her

i am the hand
me down suit
of the junkie
of the hustler
of the gigolo
of the millionaire
i am the lighter
of streetlamps
who takes off
on his nightly
rounds & never
seen from
or heard
from again
i am the kid
who keeps
on getting
thrown
out of class
& i swear just
trying to make
a connection
& show them
where i'm at
i am the son
of a dentist
who all the
hygienists
have a crush
on & can't

keep myself
out of trouble
peeing in
between
the paper
thin walls
of a split-level
in the suburbs
i am as romantic
as they come
& just as ribald
as well & only
feel content
when i cum
& cum!
& cum!
& cum!
i was in my prime
in my childhood
i was in my slide
during puberty
i am the opium
& poppy plant
seventh inning
stretch finally
falling fast
asleep by
the lapping sea
i am the peephole
peeking back

at the peeper
trying desperately
to escape reality
i am the peeling
wallpaper
of the widow
who just can't
stop weeping
i am the burnt
down rollerdisco
on my way
to the big
city unaware
i got the skate
key right in the
back pocket of
my dungarees
i am the towering
dead prehistoric
tree in the silent
holy lagoon
& when it
finally tips
& teeters
& goes
crash &
kaboom
to make
its grand
farewell

& tributary
& trail
& no one's
around to
hear its
echoing
bells did
i ever really
exist at all
cuz never
could tell
i am all those
torrents of rain
which come pouring
down in the streams
& mountains leaving
a whole blanket of
sky-blue mist spiritually
enveloping the village
turning to a
whole new
necessary
dimension
& sense of
forgiveness
& forgetting
reflective
redemption
i am the earlybird
& nightbird loitering

at lonesome window
whose warbling
like the rhythm
of brooks & rivers
brings about some
thing of a certain
kind of rebirth
i am that still fog
i am the mountain
i am the mountain
still inside fog
i am the dawn
when the draw
bridge wakes
up in the
skeleton
skyline
i am the bleary
eyed hotelier
of welfare
hotels whose
life is just as
miserable as
the drag queens
& dope addicts
& runaways
& fugitives
wanted dead
or alive who
don't give

a damn
if they're
dead or alive
i am the fallen
angel whose
been betrayed
way too many
times with an
arrow through
the heart of my
boneless spine
i am a criminal
i am a crow
i am a cow
i am the corn
i am a king
i am a clown
i am a vagabond
making out
with a girl
in the barn
i am a one-night stand
i am a pony on fire
i am an outside cat
i am an inside cat
i am a lost cat
i am a rooster
i am a hen
i am a found man
i am a bear

i am a cub
set loose
from his mom
just looking
for a spare
scrap of food
& don't have
a mean bone
in this lone
some world
roaming from
garbage can
to home
to cobble
stone
to shore
to forest
to farm &
am the talk
of the town
i am a storm
inside a bottle
i am a dream
inside a theater
i am a nightmare
in a puddle
i am a river
on the ceiling
in the chandelier
of a vacant village

i am a clocktower
in the asylum
in the locket
in the pocket
of the nostalgic
heart & soul
of a lost
& found
romantic
wanderer
i am all
that glitter
in a snowglobe
on the ledge of
a sexless sister
i am a delinquent
far kinder &
compassionate
& classier than
any classroom
kiss ass who
will cut throats
in the future
i am a lifelong
criminal on
the tightrope
between the
schoolyard
& courtyard
with my

disguise
stuffed in a
brown paper
lunch bag
in case
i don't
make it
home alive
i am the carnival
freak still fast
asleep in my
deep shallow
fetal position
nightmare
dream
passed-out
in weeping
drunken caravan
along the bullet
ridden ocean
with a porthole
view of charlton
heston planted
on knees in
loincloth
hysterical
& histrionic
holy & sacred
with sunken
standard & poor

shipwrecked soul
crawling past
the gigantic
crown & ravaging
visage of lady liberty
barely piercing shore
with broken off tinfoil
bits of the hindenburg
that brilliant beautiful
elephant electrocuted
to death in a heap of
flesh cuz got sick
of tourists tossing
cigarettes at him
& the birdman
of alcatraz still
with us in the not
too far off distance
i am the balloonist
on his deathbed
surrounded by
my fellow
acrobats
contortionists
slapstick
comedians
magicians
& madmen
i am the runaway
train with no real

destination as long
as it's running!
& running!
& running!
& running!
i am the
shadow
of the sun
with prisms
of late-noon
dust sneaking a peek
through the drunkard
stained-glass window
of the shattered souls
of the bus station
at dusk which is
the evolution
of civilization
playing hide
& go seek
with the
orphan
origins
of the
bleak
universe.

hotel x,

at my grand petite boutique hotel they gave
it a half star rating with an exclamation point
showing pictures of it always raining built
directly adjacent to a garbage dump which of
course triggers all those gorgeous panoramic
sunsets as evidenced by the dusty glossy
postcard carousel in the lobby with views
of the boardwalk and praline and peanut brittle
stands and old retired madmen and gigolos and
runaways and winos and drag queens and drug
dealers just going through their everyday rounds
of survival, while every room is haunted with
apparitions and thick faded floral curtains drawn
due to paranoia and self-deprivation and very
strange low-hanging sputtering chandeliers
framed jigsaw puzzles of crashing pastel oceans
and elvis and the signing of the declaration of
independence; none of those rare obvious and
infamous privileged suburban women showing
off their perfect health club bodies posing with
their mandated plastic ear to ear smiles, no
worries or problems with their margaritas
sunbathing by the poolside while always very
gregarious with the other socializing guests,
showing off their convenient seductive acumen
and willingness to be sluts to prove how open
and receptive they are on their all-inclusive

exclusive vacations for the sake of western
civilization, but real down and out naked
divorcees making breakfast in the cramped
up kitchenette for new much younger boyfriends
who they treat like both slave and savior and
seem content just trying to make it somewhere
between a psychotic fantasized reenactment,
rebirth and redemption, cross-dressers who
work the graveyard shift removing their makeup,
nude anorexic women tied to chairs blindfolded
smoking cigarettes getting their pictures taken
by abusive sadistic boyfriends who they thought
were artists and there to save them; the rest of
them, the front desk clerk, the doorman/bellman,
and concierge are all man-eating mannequins
with great big madman mechanical grins giving
the impression of hospitality and that they'll go
all out for you in crisis like some father figure
you never had (in the hopes to heal your fragile
and damaged soul) but in real life will act aloof
and arrogant and go into instant denial. the
cuisine will be all those fast-food joints when
the sun goes down and pass you your extra-
crispy through the revolving bulletproof screen
but if in fact willing to be adventurous and
take risks and get into the spirit and acclimate
and acculturate can take full advantage of the
ambiance and those bleak bleary-eyed half
stars blinking like mad outside your window
for all lost souls with a garden view
of the alley and sea.

why z?

eventually tv's just going to be
these screens beaming commercials
for psychotropic meds and pharmaceuticals
and all those suddenly newly discovered
disorders we've never even heard of before
(so all the corrupt drug companies can make
their dough) and sure we can't get on in this life
without one of these elixirs and cure-alls to help
us get through all the pain and suffering and
sorrow this life has inflicted on us and the tv
will just show all those safe & secure scenarios
(having a difficult time trying to figure out and
make full sense of the parable) of those middle-
aged couples maybe even sometimes some
single mom (with mania) or daughter
who can do no wrong perhaps having
their first crisis or hallucination of
disorientation or something chronic
after returning home from the hospital
happily ever after maybe first love walking
down the aisle all the exact same schnucks
showing up to the funeral while we'll have
absolutely no reason at all to leave our homes
having experienced it all from the comforts
of our living room realizing it's all just one
big long hawaii 5-0 barnaby jones charlie's
angels episode right before we enter
the pearly gates of heaven
a pair of rollerskates
slung around doorknob...

the middle ages,

i think i'm losing
it but who knows
maybe not and in fact
just finding it and have
developed something of
a fine and decent rapport
with one of the bankers
over the phone who
helps me with my
problems whenever
something's going
wrong like if my
account looks just
a little bit suspicious
like the other day
expedia without
asking my consent
debited my account
for like a thousand bucks
and she instantly ameliorated
the problem and i thanked her
and as a joke asked her if she
couldn't now maybe make the
reservation for *disney world*
and said only if i could take
her and i told her as long as
she wears the mickey mouse

ears and recently been having
this fantasy that instead of taking
a mistress and taking her to romantic
places like rome or paris or somewhere
in spain would take her to the magical
kingdom with one of those all-inclusive
rooms where people from the suburbs
all hang out buzzed and intoxicated
with tropical drinks in the middle
of the pool trying to forget their
miserable existences as she
would simply stroll all around
the room naked with those mickey
mouse ears on in some sort of
brilliant arrested stage of
development midlife crisis

a man can dream can't he
and think i may be losing
it but who knows maybe in
fact might just be finding it.

picket fences,

    i think i might be losing it
              as this morning
                        found myself
            giggling
  to *bewitched*
      & samantha was pissed
                & zapped darren
right to the sofa
    in his blue pajamas
          & blue blanket
              but thought doesn't
        seem all that bad
    as had the whole place
to himself
      with the floral sofa
         & built-in bookcases
             & garden doors
which led straight
out to the patio
   & were in a quarrel
        as darren's salesman boss
                larry
       was the one in charge
    of bulldozing
   the park
  the kids
played in

        & samantha
            & the other wives
                    decided

to just start picketing
so they might

    have a brighter
        & happier future
            while things back then

 just seemed so much more
simple & innocent
                & complicated

    with technicolor & suburbia
            & salesmen
  in sleek salesmen suits

        but i don't know
     think there's still something
  to be said

about returning home
        to your postage lamp lawn
at dusk
with all
    the manufactured
        power-struggles
that shangrila brings on

        for your token martini
    & an olive.

the ole factory senses,

1.

i ask my wife
to pick up a flower
for our shattered vase

2.

mr. wu bought
a dozen roses
for my mom

3.

she loves me she loves me not
is the denouement for those
who feel taken for granted

4.

we start planting gardens
out of a certain kind of reenactment
for purposes of rebirth and redemption.

customs,

every once in
a while my wife
likes to hang out
at the gas station
with the old men
drinking their
morning coffee
ribbing each other
while this morning
told me about the
safety inspector
with his paunch
belly and suspenders
and new buzz haircut
the other old timers
were ridiculing him
about how he was
going to scare off
all the children in
town and who
gave her a new
factoid and out
of nowhere
suddenly
told me
enthusiastically
how in alaska

they have the
largest vegetables
due to one full month
where it's sunny all day
i responded really erica
and she said yeah with
a great big proud smile
and then vanished
down the hall and
thought this was
just as relevant
and worthwhile
as anything else
i've heard in
so damn long.

right around dawn,

i like watching the local news
and when they show the weather
they always show those small towns

with those glowing sputtering streetlamps
in the deep dark night and all seems calm
and don't get why they just don't get along

ticker reads *patchy fog*
and you count your lucky
stars and losing lotto numbers.

the life & times of clark kent,

cell u liar! cell u liar!
cell u liar! cell u liar!
all these codependent
contraptions of communication
which is supposed to make
our lives so much easier
but i don't know i think
i so much more preferred
that telephone booth
on the corner of 14th
in union square when
i used to drop a dime
in the slot & only had
a certain amount of
time to spare & try
& charm & get her
& it was always how
many dimes i had left
when i reached deep
down in jean pocket
& how much time
jammed in that
phone booth
charming &
schmoozing
with ethereal
snow coming

down building
up to a great big
blizzard on 14th
& 3rd not even
being aware of it
& you eventually
get her & means
so much more
than one of
those cookie
cutter commercialized
razor-thin self-important
wannabe contraptions am
just saying sometimes like
nietszche said the journey
or maybe just the effort
& challenge proves
to be worth it & has
so much more meaning.

how to cut grass,

odd amount of pride america
puts into such things like tv
and technology and certain
ceremonies like the rose bowl
parade putting your faith into
the stars or gods or the *goodyear*
blimp working 30 years 10 hour days
slaving for some insurance company
up on top of a hill they treat like some
castle or holy cathedral (this is what they
refer to as married to their jobs and *must*
be good family men, yeah right!) sneaking out
of some suburban dead end when the sun rises
with the sad solitary dew still on the grass as
nothing could be more solemn or silent with
a bag stuffed with golf clubs clinging onto
your last vestige of sanity having popped
out your token 2 ½ kids and a wife who
hasn't been touched in years (who now
bends over routinely doggie-style for
the neighbor next door every chance
she gets in some vain attempt
to try and attract his attention)
driving blindly bumpadabumpa
home after a 12 hour day as a
civil engineer past the lit-up dog
track & mall just in time to drag

the garbage cans at the end of
the driveway at the end of the day
into some safe & secure garage
perfectly organized which might
guarantee a box seat in heaven or at
least have something a little cleaner
& neater & tidier than your neighbor.

depression the situational kind,

people will just drain
the hell out of you
and make you
want to pull
your brain
straight
out
your
skull
like
young
frank
en
stein
or in
spector
cluseau
& still
not leave
you the
hell alone
when just
want to be
left alone
on the
morning
of the

apocalypse
with your
scone
& cup
of tea
listening
through
the static
of old time radio
to some commercial
for a used car lot
on miracle mile
once i was
alone i was
petrified.

a different form of blue,

these days i find myself
out of nowhere just
singing songs like–

o lord will you buy
me a mercedes-benz
my friends all have porsches

people like the game warden
on the other end of the phone
suddenly picking up going–
hello? hello? is there...

you deep down inside
really knowing no.

the team to trust,

today i got eaten up by the weather woman.
she just stuck her head straight through the tv
and suddenly gobbled me up with that great ear
to ear photogenic smile, fangs, and big gums,
as i tumbled down her throat down her lovely
trachea and right into her tummy all in one gulp
and i gotta tell you really caught me off guard
while she continued on with her report pointing
to the heartland, lower valley, lake eerie, rio
grande, sioux falls, mississippi...those idiot
bicyclists continuing to race past my window
in their spandex racing uniforms bike helmets
and very safe and secure mandated reflectors

i wonder if at the apocalypse
they'll offer endless shrimp

can see where disney & ibm
are up about a quarter point.

on character and reliability,

i had a revelation this evening
helping my wife make dinner
for my kid breaking open the
chef boy ardee then suddenly
it hit me and realized pouring
it out of the can it never goes
bad; those perfectly square
raviolis which hit the spot
what me and my friends
always turned to while
growing up and just
standing there tonight
in the kitchen pouring
it into a bowl realized
chef boy ardee the only
one in this life i can
rely on and who has
never let me down.

all the good little monsters,

1

clutching onto her reading bifocals
he scampers into the bathroom and
swings opens the shower door
and declares–*grandma! you
forgot these!* –o sweetie

2

this morning my teenage son told me—
*don't ever make me listen to rick ashley's
never gonna give you up…it actually makes
my ears bleed.* i answered–*put barry white
on your screen* and we just naturally closed
our eyes and started bopping our heads to the
beat then he just picked up his laptop with
chicken legs in his underwear and disappeared
down the stairs going–*that was hip, ain't never
gonna give you up*

3

whenever my son has play dates
down in the basement i find myself
naturally humming–*if you want to
view paradise* and then his friends
ask–*what the hell is that?* and
he naturally responds–*that's just
my dad who likes to pretend he's
willie wonka in the chocolate factory*
"o" and then go back to their wrestling

4

in the morning laying out on our green gushy
couch dylan just naturally spouts–*today we're
gonna dissect a sheep's eye* which to me was
so keen and brilliant and what kids are famous
for in no need of a response and practically
said it all.

dissecting a sheep's eye,

let me tell you about the time i dissected a
sheep's eye. it was around 2:00 during mrs.
kendall's science class when we were being
taught a unit about the eye.

i chose brody to be my observer who instantly
strapped on a pair of goggles and white lab
coat. i chose a scalpel and without fear
got right in there.

we had to make some incisions in the cornea
as i split the eye in half. out came the fluid.
and when we peeled off the retina we could
signify the color of the sheep's eye. but...

the eye was carcinogenic and it possibly got
on me so that led to a certain amount of concern.

but me and brody were pretty calm during the
whole procedure. everyone else was white with
fright and screaming out loud when the fluid
got on them. i myself a bit bugged-out that
i was poisoned so i started yakking about
my misconception to mom and dad who
disproved my theorem.

after mom went food shopping and picked
me up i got straight into the shower and
showered everything off.

a different sort of proof,

birds with baubles on
badgering outside panes–
maybe! maybe! maybe! maybe!

kids returning home aimlessly
mischievously the last day
of school first day of holy

sacred action & adventure
summer; a strange early
amorphous buzzing

of crickets and cicadas
wandering up neverending
long lavish hills of the suburbs

thankfully with no real
destination infamous outlaws
or heroes returning from war

no longer having to figure out
word problems, mathematical
proofs, logarithms, irregular verbs

that sense of finally
at last it's all over
with no more

sense of the past
or future and nothing
and everything to live for

in no
par tickle
you order

getting laid,
pool hopping,
bags of marijuana…

american haiku,

wow that whole summer
with golf clubs slung
over shoulder

for those
miserable
wallstreeters

but getting bronzed
and more muscular
all you ever heard

when you turned
on the radio
on the rock

'n roll station
in oldsmobile
stationwagon

was *eyes*
without
a face

by billy idol
just a simple
tee and blue

jeans
wow
older

sisters
starting
to flirt with me

in late-evening
barrooms starting
to make a name

the only rumors
which meant
a thing...

the weather: munday,

the delinquents & studs with shirts off
always come out at dusk riding their
bicycles like mad into the mist of
mountains just like the deer & cub

not by coincidence looking back & reflecting
about your childhood this is when you
were most alive and had the most
spirit and learned the most

everything after that not exactly sure…

the weather: toosday,

i don't know
    some freakin people
        just seem to have it
            so damn easy

    like that pretty
        little weather woman
      in her tasteless sleazy

  sequined skirt
& red ruby slippers

    casually pointing to just another
        one of those western wildfires

which got ignited in california
    this one discovered
        to have started
            from a simple spark
      from a flat tire

    & there she stands
        with that sparkling *dentyne* smile

all higher-than-holy
    like some church girl in a choir
        (who has slain millions

                                of men
        through seduction & betrayal)
                                while you find your
                                self on a daily basis

                        in the daily struggle
                    having to fight
        the bad weather

                        the humidity & hail & holy
                                mother of jesus
                                        forced to have
        to explain yourself
        to some corrupt little schmuck
                                        insurance man
                        with a napoleonic complex
                            who all he cares about
                                        is facts & figures

        having devoted
                    your whole damn existence
                        climbing multiple ruins & pyramids

                        muttering to yourself
                    self-made man-made mantras
        just to keep your head together

                        turned-out, taking that ferry
                                        through the bleak

                        eternal evening
          to all those lost islands
of atlantis

     which just suddenly sank
            to the bottom of the sea
with absolutely no explanation.

the weather: whensday,

my god what has happened
              to the state of florida?

     when i was a child we'd get all excited
to visit
     the magical kingdom
          with our brand new
                pair of leather-
     suede *pumas*

& now they got these gunmen
          these gunchildren
               waltzing into schools

with whole arsenals
of aok rifles & hand grenades

ready to launch at the student body
          for payback for alien
               hating & bullying.

you met your first girlfriend
          down in key biscayne
              at that pristine hot

while every night
    in that dim corny lounge
        the same balding middle-aged
                lounge singer

would croon out loud
the same song–
i love you
    just the way you are

loving the feeling
    of pretending to be in love.

the weather: thirsty,

in the solitary summer evening
the firefly flickers like a candlelit
messenger, like some bright beacon
with his anatomy full of fire fleshing
out weeding out the good from the liars

you sit back wasted wired having driven all over
the state of rhode island having visited all those
abandoned children in all those group homes
& shelters, just helping to maintain knowing
for the time being ain't gonna get much better

taking that bridge back & forth from newport
to providence like some *myth of sysiphus*
cabdriver or k. in *the castle* during that
interminable journey going round
& round not getting any closer

knowing deep down inside
all you can really rely on
is the flashing fleeting
& transient images of the
brilliant blazing here & now

crows in backyard
stealing all your corn
like fireworks halfway
sprung open leaving it
feeling futile & forlorn.

the weather: frieday,

thunder rumbles in over the mountains right
before the traveling carnival and the trail of
echoes from the speakers reminding all citizens
to evacuate in a kind and civil and courteous
manner from family swim while a jostling
juggernaut of lively blissful freaks make
their journey down the side of the glistening
purple road when rain starts to fall and breaks
the humidity cleaning the air and stirring up
all the sacred spirits of old. you are not sure
whether to turn to the medicine cabinet or the
shot bottles of rum chilling in the refrigerator
which will turn you into one of those lone
solitary heroes from one those westerns
exiting the movie theater in the midst of
puddles; what's most important of all is
young secret romance going down in the
cobblestone alley of the tavern which
leads to the silhouetted steeples and
mountains. you imagine a giraffe sticking
his head out the window of a caravan
contented vanishing into the darkness.

an ancient study of contemporary
culture in america,

a young jack nicholson & art garfunkel
                scrubbing in the shower
                                in college
                rapping about women
        most notably
                candice bergen
                        showing later on
                                in the film
                in later life
                        their growth
                                & development
                & evolution
    (regression)
                in the swinging seventies
                        in the business world
                                of new york city
        with their chauvinistic views
                of the female species
there was that film *love story*
                & what's his name
                        in the *paper chase*
        after sick of being humiliated
                        disgraced & brow-beaten
by john houseman
                in harvard law school
                        flipping the tables on him

& bawling him out
these movies seeming to have
the theme & mood & hue of
the mercurial season of fall

in real life a good pal
of mine who we both

used to drive taxis
       told me the story
              how coincidentally
                    at separate times
picked up lucille ball
       & she chinced
              him with a quarter...

one of those love letters you
hate to write during marriage,

just wanted to bring to your attention because
i think important for you to know as just
think sometimes just forget i'm the one
who always mentions it would be great if
somehow we could figure out a way each year
of going to the caribbean and however we save it,
some people find interesting ways of doing it,
i'd love it, weather it's from our taxes or even
a bond here or there as think we only go around
once and every single one doesn't have to be
saved for a rainy day; it's important for you
to know and hopefully you're mature and
compassionate and sensitive enough to know
why i'm writing this, and how some of the
things you said yesterday can really be damaging
to the ego and identity, when i was working
those mad hours, all i wanted to do was travel
with you, whether it was europe a couple times
or ireland or gloucester or white water rafting out
in maine, again right when i got paid it became a
natural instinct and tradition and loved doing it
going to the silver city galleria literally that
morning when i got my paycheck and would be
in the kids clothing shop spending at least $100
on dylan then would usually get you something
as well from *old navy,* that really meant some-
thing to me and meant the world to me, and

would spend close to an hour in there before
i saw my first clients...steve and bill would
always ask me to go to the strip club after
work and told them out of respect for you from
what you had been through with your father and
my love and respect for you just couldn't as well
as just loved my new life and was excited just to
return home; from where we used to live in that
god awful association while other clinicians on
my team lived right there around the clinic,
i'd be the first one in the schools and be there
already by like eight o'clock, had the highest
and largest caseload, and saw up to 10 clients
a day (actually developed really good relation-
ships with the secretaries with my sense of
humor and principles and vice principles)
which was close to the maximum quota
including clients i saw after school clinic-
based; you kept on telling me to quit cause
you knew i was miserable and exhausted
and couldn't stand my supervisor but if you
remember me saying there is no way i'm quitting
cause of how long it had taken me to ramp up
my caseload of clients and reputation with the
caregivers and parents and didn't know the next
time or opportunity i'd get; that morning when
you had me go to providence and just didn't
want to go to another dr's appointment as felt it
gratuitous you made me drive you there because
you said you did not know how to get there and

worried about the drive; i said out of sheer
responsibility and diligence well let me still see
some of my clients and literally drove all the way
in the opposite direction to the taunton middle
school to see them, please never forget this, my
hard work and perseverance whenever i am
afforded the opportunity to see clients or
build up a caseload, if you remember literally for
the first 6 months there they gave me like only
a couple almost as if testing me or for whatever
political reason and worked for that horrible
bitch at fst; a similar example, when my father
was told to declare bankruptcy in the mid 70's
because of his dealings with another father on
our block in wall street and knew he was making
money illegally still stayed with him because his
logic was that he was making quick money for
him and as long as he kept making him profits
didn't care how he did it; when he eventually
got nailed for insider-trading all of his lawyers
told him to declare bankruptcy, and he said
absolutely not and ended up working like
14 hour days, but at least had a practice
which he owned where he could always
see patients because of course that's just the
nature of the business, yet again he did very
risky things and paid for it with 3 young kids
and felt an extreme amount of guilt about it,
again i would implore you to look at my past
and my work habits and the huge caseload i

took on even though was overworked for years and exhausted and drained and how after getting unjustly fired due to a medical appointment didn't even want to be at still tried my best and damndest whether later on it was working at a methadone clinic in freezing new bedford in the winter at 4:30 in the morning when the dope addicts took their dosing's and can't tell you how depressing it was with you and dylan still sleeping driving down the highway in the deep darkness and a frozen cold empty office, that job i took all the way out in plymouth making pretty good money but the insane sadistic slavedriver i had to work with, then finding another job working for the town of new bedford where she promised me a position and while signing up doing paper work shiesty illegally ran into another lady who said that girl didn't have the authority to hire me and i was fucked and there was no going back; there was another job i was about to get for dss and when she asked for a recommendation from that idiot supervisor said i was a good social worker but wouldn't hire me; you remember that! of course being the compulsive liar he was, told me he gave me a good recommendation when i ran into him at *planet fitness* and i finally called him out on it and he tried to squirm out of it, the coward that he was. again, you know i'd do practically anything, things you wouldn't even think of, from standing

all day as a bellman at my age in a resort in
essex, to delivering pharmaceuticals in the wee
hours of the morning all over vermont until i got
lost in the mountains with the crazy howling
dogs not being able to find those clinics
because they didn't train me on those routes,
to *red hen bakery* which i tried multiple times
but just couldn't stand for all those hours stuffing
bread due to my condition, to the recent interviews
which i told you about in depth where i
was there for hours on end and still didn't have
the respect to call me back; again just wanted to
reiterate these things from a fair and sensitive
and honest and compassionate place and know
i'm always the one trying to come up with new
ideas because i feel it is so important for the
family's sake like maybe puerto rico on *expedia*
or cozumel also too which can get great rates or
even las vegas where can get unbelievable deals,
but really nice warm desert weather and big
beautiful rooms and good gourmet food just to
change things up a little, and believe strongly
honestly where there's a will there's always a way,
like for example in vegas can get plane
and hotel for like $1,500 all together, same thing
with like puerto rico all-inclusive or costa rica,
i had mentioned before disney world driving
there, but you completely blew me off and told
me you couldn't because of your vertigo; and
yeah i guess couldn't exactly imagine myself

because of my deep loathing for tourists in
what'cha'ma'call magical kingdom or walking
down what's that memory lane to a place like it's
a small world after all or like those spinning
teacups or flying dumbo but you know you could
do it if really wanted and i sure could find a way
of keeping myself busy during the day in the
sunshine state of orlando, and if you really
wanted to do it with the family and sincere
about it know we could find certain ways
of saving, hopefully you'll take this letter
in good faith and from a good place and out
of love and respect from me because that's
where i'm sincerely coming from, and so
really truly like and appreciate and thank you
how you did try to break up the quarrel yesterday
and liked where you were going when you
said how you used to like to wait at home for
me and prepare a good home-cooked meal and
so on because those are straight-up some
compassionate and beautiful and heartwarming
images and moments and trust me these days i
do think of them often even though of course
in real life, not too realistic considering the
madness of what i was doing pretty much
going through the motions, even that first job
literally driving all over the state of rhode island
from group home to shelter to clinics all day
exhausted being completely drained felt more
like a taxi driver which of course you know

i used to do back in the day graveyard shift
in nyc, didn't know i used to just eat lunch
by myself up on top of the bay in newport
while still listening to sports radio from new
york just past those ole time mansions
they called the cottages on the precipices
overlooking the crashing ocean and dreaming
about the future lots of love and do hope
you understand and believe what i am saying
here reiterating things all the god's honest truth
thanks again for reading love joey…

brazil, brazil

davey crocket in his coonskin cap
                laid-back
      in the fetal position
    after nodding-out
on a bundle of heroin
        in the magical kingdom
                      hallucinating
  he's troy donahue
        on the beach
             no more in conflict
with the ridiculous & oppressive
        guilt & shame & norms
                of society
(living one of those real-life sci-fi horror films
        he has gotten used to
& ac/cult/u/rated)

        & being a natural die/hard romantic
when all the technicolor waves cum rushing
    in while dreams he clicks opens up one
                of those pieces
of leisure luggage & there's a fresh clean
        sky-blue buttondown businessman
shortsleeve shirt
      a pair of khakis
straw hat & saddle shoes

                    when he finally awakes
in this strange quasi
magical kingdom
                he'll order a free dvd
        for life insurance, faith
            & home security

        to keep the dream of martinis
                            one of those
contemporary split-levels
            & beauty of safe & secure

suburbia alive
                    might even be that motel
    room
at the end of the tracks
        in reno
                    stumbling out
at 7 in the morning
already 83 degrees

having spent the evening
                    listening to the bums
        & winos
crashing their bottles
                        against the traintracks
                but just like everything else
        gotta get up
    the way
        he was raised
            & grew up–*brazil, brazil...*

51 poor traits,

1. fools rushin for gold:en the night

2. amerikas been way too glamorized

3. specially those punks on motorbikes

4. rather take black boy on his unicycle
racing gracefully mutely hustling threw
harloom on sweltering psalmer's day

5. robert frawst racing k. sandburg
in potato sak race

6. i ain't kidin they dun make movies in amerika
no mojust recycled formulaic crapolo while chuck d
posed who stole the soul & he was correctamundo

7. whir always tawt to observe postkards
slowly sensitivaly of madisse & magreet

8. if not would be kicked out of
kar on the way to applepicking

9. to see that family of farmers with fine
wild boys always with the high voices
hi yup in the mowntin

10. cawed *sky farm*

11. the tour bus of old timers always
turned upsidedown on sigh of road

12. roadkill always sincerely felt so bad
for who didn't quiet make it nigh before

13. that tavern where they serve four
different swords of raabit & sweet
breads & succulent black brandy

14. sometimes i dream i just was one of
those strange sexual identities & opened
up some modest flamboyant french bistro

15. inn the heart of flickring boojoise farest
looking like a vase turned upsidedown
over a hole mess of clandestine flowers
at sundown from a mister to his misstress

16. where skolars & rumantics cud have quick
secret randy-voos on the border of smoke
stacks & synogog

17. (sounding like the kross of a foghorn & shofar
pronownced showfur with thick
queens accent

18. the life & times of the swirling ocean
of the hx of evolution echwing deep
within the inside of a conch shell

19. like the leftover drumsticks of some
burntout burlesque drummer playing
drumroll for the punchlies of some
dummy-ventriloquist playged with
multawpall personality disorder)

20.til you suddenly realize women
have been whimsicall & whisperin
& gigglin & seducin haven a damn
fine time since thee beginintime in
their lace curtain chimin berth inn
that steam locomotive barreling through
manifestdestinymidnights getting out &
seducing that poorlone crooningcowboy
bye the campfire & before you know it
has him all lassoed&deckedout in his
tuxedo on their weddingnight traipsing
down the long staircase of his grand log
cabin to his wiseass comicalcowboy
palsintengallons wit explodincigars

21.been doing this since theeorigins of time
that ole classic black&white movie leftover
on your insomniatelevision from previous
night until you suddenly realize it's all
just porkchops&baked apples&onions
with a touch of brandy or cooking wine
which goes right to the batteredheart&soul

22.the rippling aroma of formaldehyde
streaming from the scarlet senorita curtains
at south brooklyn casket until you suddenly
realize it's all just a jung brando & james
dean & even omar shariff that we're all just
brando & james dean & a jung omar shareef

23. merkreal chain of seasons
not sure witch one into witch
like a boy swiping at invisible
butterflies in the morning mist

24. the wildapples already fall
in off the windswept branches

25.thee raydio jus deklares–
pan-seared... gowin
into thee week/end

26.flashinglightsonewspaperman
crawlingthrutheedeepdarkmountin

27.the tinbarn becomes tin again

28.& thebrokenbones of brokenmen
start dreaming of wildinsanecarolinas
those hangingmoss antebellumislands
takingoff in the deepdarknight from thee
appalachians threw the glowing outskirts
of philadelphia brilliantsacredhistorical

pillars of broodingpresidents in hour
nationscapitol ole civilwar ghetto of
richmondvirginia&blearyeyedbeaming

29.sunstarts rising whencrossin the mason
dixon litrally starting to smell the sprinkled
dew of stamens o' fragrant magnolia&crepe
myrtle & the strangesaintlyspirits of young
confederatesoldiers weirdwildwestvirginia
to the suddenswamp of thee outerbanks
&killdevilhills where wilbur & orville
made their courageous acrobatic moves &took
theirone giantleap faw mankind with sputtering
modelgluepropellers toholyhorizons

30.snowmelt beggin inn theepurplysyrupy hills
magically bringing the maddeningswollenrivers
back to life again and the redpickups witloads
of splitfirewood zooming down bluebeaming
roads to holyfairytale longlost dustynations

31. crosscountryskis leaned up
gainst great burning crackling fire
with the stray nostalgik aroma of ole
time skiwax & chocolate nut fruit bars

32. gorjist impovershed girls
serving steaming buns...

167

33. developed a taste (an hankering)
for karamel apples & bakde stuff shrimp
& chocolate pekan pie at *the red lion inn*

34. later on ironikilly with runaway divorcees
who'd been underpreciated)or mistreated(inn
carcerated having the greatest affairs of all time

35. reskewing them from the night
mare suburbancrimeof life
& their skowling ancestors
& a (long) life of crumb

36. [heart my wife to death even tho
she's far mo violent & impulsive
mortality measured by the
moida-rate o homo-sapiens

37. best that we can do for a wife
is check up on her ask how she's
doing listen to every one of her
stories all her sobbing validate
her hug her go all out for her
tell her she looks cute & good
& like her bun buy her sundresses
from the bottom of your heart that
chinese buffet when you can afford it
thank her for a nice warm meal thank
her for a nice warm meal thank her for
a nice warm meal for putting up with
you when all you want to do at the end

of the day is put a bullet in your brain
& know the only thing that can save
you is a baseball game & if don't get
any of these things in return guess just
learn to accept this double standard &
the difference & remainder of the sexes]

38. that fight or flee ritual & tradition like some
mad religion of cheeseburgers & fries & koke-kola
at *the red rooster* right by mini golf & the
insane asylum where rich boys always havent
tempertantrums on dismissive fathers

39. at boxcar diners the last stop on the railroad
doing their token visit from the upper ease sigh

40. like jesus christ being crucified against
that cat's kradle made out of colorful yarn

41. that red haird girl i fell in love wit
who used to be tied naked against a chair
& piktures taken of her by her sadistik boy
fiend always making the wrong choice in men

42. now stranded with a form of sitwaytional
deepression or some plane eternally kafkaeskilly
stuck on the runwaysome ufo with just no desire
to take off cuz the aliens got othritis & now
addicted to painkiller content to live happily
ever after with the gardening equipment
beneath the porch

43. the scarecrow & santa claws...

44. survived id awe constantly on,the, run
misstaken for some sort of kriminal of sorts
even treated far worse

45. with a backpack on the back of my
back filled with paper backs by kerouac
& burrows & keats & shelley & witgunsteen
& spinoza & dawtoevsky the sorrows of jung
werther & fear of trembling by gurtter every
last single one of pound's obsessivekantos to
eventually become an infamous unsung artist
not who they thought i was as the most wanted
feeling mostly unwanted

46. when they no longer wanted
me dozing-off in the bellman's closet
during a graveyard in the luxry ho/tell buzzness

47. swear used to sleep like drakula with one eye
open in the grandfather clock like clockwork
right by the un used woodpile beneath thee
creaking beaming stars

48. (wear thee only sound u'd hear
was the woodpecker pounding his
bill again the barn as a maiden call)

49. high off mom's undrunk wine
to try & maintain my buzz
& avoid nightmares

50. blow out the chandelier

51. in the mist of
midnight mantras

on the nature of wild turkey,

scuttling down the hill
of your backyard yakking
like a posse of old yiddish
ladies from jamaica, queens
who will be served on a gigantic
platter in their mu-mus and curlers
and wise ass grandson getting tipsy
for the first time high on *manishewitz*
wine convinced he has fallen in love
with the puerto rican girls in the kitchen
who giggle and feel flattered feeding into it

he sits back in his stepmom's
oldsmobile station wagon buzzed
and nursing his high daydreaming
late at night heading home down
the long island expressway realizing
at a very young age it all just really has
to just do with moments and trying to
make them last as long as possible.

for t. bickle,

who would think
    back then in those crazy
        & complicated times
            with a frisbee

full of weed
    on top of the refrigerator
        in that last forgotten house
            at the end
        of the boardwalk
in coney island
when driving a cab
    graveyard in manhattan
        & that mad hatter statistic

of one cab driver
    getting killed a week
  for some reason

    maybe just to keep
      up my toughness
        & killer instincts

would creep into my window
    with the sun rising
      drained at the end
  of some long insane shift
in the streets

     completely empty
       like the neon
draining
from that old rickety
rollercoaster
  would just sit back
     in my corduroy easy chair
       reading the stats

from the night before
   with a bag of mix fruit & nuts
      & tall can of beer

vegging-out
to the brilliant jams
of the allman brothers

   fillmore east

 the stray melancholy waves
    crashing in the distance
      keeping the beat

somehow subliminally
part of the same
    soundtrack & scene

  would be some of the most intriguing
       of times

    & something i look back at
with absolutely no regret

        something really to be said
            about the depth
of loneliness
    about being existentially
stranded
like a piece of driftwood

washed-up along shore
    about being so angry

        having absolutely
           no fear of anything
    or anyone

& would throw down
practically anywhere
           to protect my dignity
    & honor
      deep down inside
        knowing that's
          all i had not giving

a damn
& knew could take care...

brainwash or profiles in cowardice,

america one great big
mickey mouse club
with spoiled brats
with their cameras
and smart phones
hollering like mad from
the histrionic flamboyant
pits of the award show
at their sequined idols
texting away like crazy
begging their savior for
salvation and get a busy
signal as no one there
for their man for their
borderline girlfriend
driving them mad
and all have the
exact same breakdown
and body language
and cookie-cutter
reaction a cross
between the projects
and politicians who
just don't give a damn
in their safe and secure

comfortable cozy mansions
deciding on whether...and what
will be the repercussions if they
happen to vote on a bill which
apologizes and first time ever
say sorry (just not in their
alpha-male dominating
d.n.a.) for that phase of
slavery still conveniently
try to rationalize and block
from their psyched-up psyche
(finally at last got the proper
protocol for the rock
'em sock 'em
all-american hero
who suffers from
concussions
don't know
who they are
anymore my name is
elmer fudd) hey listen!
hey did you hear the one?
the third one from ironically
the majority? minority?
whip is that what they
call or something to
that effect? still has
speaker of the house

support; god want
to talk about some
sort of fucked-up
sadistic dysfunctional
household? avon lady
also a member
of the club
used to give
speeches
fund raisers
at david duke
luncheons
and now
claims he
didn't know
who they were
where he was?
(plead the fifth?
ignorance?
concussion?)
and if you believe
that one i got a bridge
did you hear the one?
hey babe did you
iron my mask
and gown?
have you
seen my

cross?
my gun?
bowling ball?
always like
some poor
drunken punch
line at the expense
at the sacrifice &
slaughter of others.

III.

loVe sonNets
tO A tIme forGotten

somewhere around the early seventies,

there wasn't anything wrong with every friday
night as a kid watching the *brady bunch*
and then the *partridge family*

there was nothing wrong a little later on
watching the *love boat* and *fantasy island*
whose purpose was to teach us a ridiculous

life lesson and eventually
provide us hope
for the future

where
the climax
and resolved conflict

was all narrated
by meryl steubing
and ricardo montalban.

somewhere in between was
the mod squad and *charlie's angels*
not exactly sure what that had to do

with anything lying back in that little patch
of backyard in the suburbs with our thick
movie star sunglasses on and large menu

of tinfoil wide open
in front of our faces
to make us look more

sophisticated for sweet 16's
and bar-mitzvahs and
summer camp reunions

taboo to talk about those pretty rich cousins
who had turned into junkies and spoiled
daughters next door you grew up with

(there always felt something
so incestuous about it or more
so just intimate and affectionate)

who you always thought so gorgeous
with their ability to be color-coordinated
and match their sky-blue evening gowns

with sky-blue eye shadow
their suntans and bright
white high heels

whose parents bought them
a condo in the upper east side
and still couldn't get away from

all the drama; from still doing bong hits
or gigolos who they thought they had fallen in
love with and ended swindling them for all their savings

like *mets* games that went on forever
and knew they'd always find
a way of blowing it…

self-portrait (of a boy who gets his
heart broken at a bar-mitzvah),

those girls who broke your heart
at bar-mitzvahs
in the end it's all those girls
who broke your heart
at bar-mitzvahs
everyday is a girl
who broke your heart
at a bar-mitzvah...

my mom used to always claim
you're never gonna find someone
who cares about you as much as us
while always found that to be so
pompous and such an arrogant
phrase and proclamation because
in fact i did find a number of
them yet still somehow looking

those girls who are like a bouquet
of plastic flowers who you
pathetically melodramatically
declared your love for but still
somehow managed to
break your heart
at bar-mitzvahs.

your local tour guide,

one day i'm gonna just take over one of those
tour buses with a pistol and show them my past
existence and what it's all really about all the
best joints in the lower east side to get shots
of saki pints of orange *cool breeze* when that's
all you can afford and like some polite street
urchin maitr'd ask if you want it chilled sticking
it in that liquid nitrogen hot ice machine then
wrap it delicately in a brown paper bag so
you and your buddies can be wild and really
sincerely get to know all the madmen on the
avenue more than most family members
and forget it all those tenements on avenue c
to pick up your bag of d sitting all day at night
brooding romantically at *vazack's drinking
tavern* full of bartenders just trying to make
it and some do and see them later on in
independents (going what the fuck isn't…)
the other bartenders making quick under the
table exchanges while old timers getting hand
jobs from barely legal innocent angels from
the neighborhood *odessa's diner* you'd sit in
all day just reflecting and ruminating and
contemplating in the window with your
combination platter and constant glasses
of seltzer watching all your ancestors and
acquaintances just trying to get by on a daily

basis whether it's drug dealing or hooking or
working in pharmacies and driving trucks at
dawn for the ny times *tompkins square park*
where you knew the old distinguished black
men in their white beards who used to be
famous artists at *the metropolitan* other pals now
phantoms who literally got stabbed to death with
rusty screwdrivers squatters who took over those
burntout abandoned buildings through thick and
thin season after season for almost every reason
you could possibly imagine most likely due
to some form of abuse or neglect or broken
childhood or childhood they just never had
seraphim girls sharing their poems with me
scribbled on looseleaf paper erotic lovely
deep sitting all day in half-crazed cafes in
their burgundy suede vests and better than
anything i ever heard or sold in the big
sell-out bookstores wanting to get with
them and spend a one-night stand or whole
life with them and take them back to my
apartment where lucky lusciano i swear got
his start but just vanishing like everything else
on a dim overcast day in winter with all the old
puerto ricans just trying to get away from their
wives domestic life day to day struggle missing
the old country and fishing at night under the
bridges of the east river with a silhouetted view
of brooklyn taking off with my pawnshop pistol
hollering forget about it and seeing them all
wave from the windows.

warho,

no atheists added
23% more almonds
we've lived in so many places
sometimes i forget where we live
and have to turn on the local cable
and watch girl's high school basketball
and turn on the used-car commercials
as well and know exactly where i am
(insane ponytails swinging like mad
like being whimsically whipped against
the skin and think they'll make like
beautiful portuguese or sicilian wives
one day while the newly-waxed courts
are always so clean and beaming like
someone just finishing with the zamboni
and the stands are always empty and the
referees are like these overcompensating
accountant perverts or hobby shop owner
sex addicts whose wives all left them and
their older moms from new england just
sitting in the aisles scowling as security)
when we first moved out here used to watch
this co-ed hockey as they'd go running up
and down the gymnasium in their sneakers
and i'd wonder where was the checking and
when would the fights break open surviving
simply off seltzer with the mountain rains
coming down in torrents and window
left open to the windy white curtains.

visit from parents in the berkshires
in the form of communication log,

1. nymphomaniac blonde-haired girl to die for in
cut-off jeans torturing her own dad & seducing
other young men & fathers at *the von trap
gardens* way up on top of the world

2. julie andrews playing hard to get *hard* to get
hard to get? & bet in bed not particularly good
cuz cares more about her image & how she
looks in mirror

3. while teenage lolita has more control than any
phony-baloney money-grubbing tourist trying
to overcompensate with luxury car

4. playing miniature golf in stowe, vt

5. very much during the months
of *twilight zone* global warming

6. bumpadabumpa with streets
ripped-up sand flying around

7. grandma comes down with major nose bleed
& takes care of it by sitting down on tourist
bench while old timer with long white beard
just starts hammering away at bench &
gives advice of how to prop her nose up

8. dad with memory loss gives nonstop advice
on how she should hold miniature golf club

9. wife heaving nonstop not quite
making it to the tourist toilets

10. 13 year old son who has absolutely no hx
of any sort of behavioral problem takes club
(most likely due to all the chaos around him)
& flings it over the hedge into the street &

11. upon retrieving it grandpa left alone not
exactly sure where he is lots of love with a
smile on his face hitting golf ball with cane
life of an overworked dentist

12. as an escape you imagine picking up
a red-haired girl hitchhiking along the side
of the road picking up her shirt to attract
me right by the homemade pie stand

13. most likely won't do supper tonight at the bar
& grill in the hotel & provide option to have son
have take-out in their room or everyone just lay
low and they can check out the new korean
or farm to table...

proof of non-existence,

last night some time during some great big fight
something they sometimes seem to thrive off
my wife going in for the kill meanly accused
me of being a waste of sperm but something
like that pearl jam song by eddie vedder who
cried out–*all i taught her was everything...*
well then what exactly would that make her?
i know she didn't mean anything by it but
like freud said there's pretty much meaning
in everything and deep-down inside really
believe she meant it

ran into an old buddy of mine the other day
from our days at *wurzweiler school of social
work,* ezra schmutz, a pretty nice decent guy
from brooklyn who only a couple years later
told me he and his wife were getting a divorce
and left me with the pithy phrase of–*i guess
i just couldn't make her happy* which seemed
more like some sort of convenient built-in
excuse or rationalization or advertisement
he neatly left with acquaintances not sure
how much he really believed this

but the one thing i know
and the one thing i'm sure
of are all those little things
in life which somehow just
painfully seem to stay with you.

living the life,

i remember catching one of my friend's older
brothers jerking-off in his room right around
the advent of cable while i was simply looking
for the bathroom somewhere off the rear set of
stairs; i swear eventually became one of those
ultra-orthodox rabbis with a wife and multiple
kids in the holy land of israel; the other brother
became a cut-throat lawyer and his mom,
married many years to a summer camp director
turned lesbian, and it all felt real secret and
hidden with this constant code of silence, like
having a serious drug problem and finally
being exposed and caught after knocking
off a pharmacy at dusk with a clear mask
in the suburbs and everyone acting shocked.

what the stats don't tell you,

we're all just
barely hanging on
just barely making it
& can attest to it
baking from it
from all this
goddamn
twilight zone
global warming shit
they say the latest
rate of suicide
skyrocketed
& shot up
in america
because of
it & in fact
find it so
much more
difficult to
get out of
bed in the
morning
to fall asleep
& nod-out
in the evening
to ole classic
movies with

movie stars
like rock hudson
edward g. robinson
kathryn hepburn
your pals freaks
buddies from
brooklyn who
literally said
how they were
just laying there
on their bed
like maybe a
whole sunday
staring up
at the ceiling
contemplating
suicide & leaving
them a message
about how much
you loved their plays
& how it remotivated
them to keep going
pals from oklahoma
& detroit, michigan
whose girlfriends
just up & left them
cuz claimed they're
inability to be there
for them & just
too insensitive

friends you grew
up with found
dead in alleys
in st. louis
which you
are sure
in retrospect
got absolutely
nothing to do
with it with this
whole goddamn
global warming
shit but just that
one little pesky thing
they just couldn't get
rid of or rebound from
& just kept on haunting
them & caused their lives
to go in a hole other direction
is there some sort of sanity wipe
to drop on this whole damn planet
like when you used to go to one
of those ole time chinese restaurants
& they'd show up like some sort of
savior with those wet warm towels
in tongs & wipe yourself down?

rush hour,

i want to sleep
side by side
with the weather
lady her heart
shaped ass
and violin
case body
her back
up and
bumpa
duh
bumpa
how she
blows then
whispering
sweet nothings
will be a nor'
easter storm
coming in from
the ohio valley
her having just
been on top
of me her
peeks and
valleys her
peaking and
me valeting

raining
and pouring
down on me
like crazy
having
finally
lost all
control
letting
it all go
and in
that one
ecstatic
moment
finally
getting
it all.

a much older young teddy roosevelt,

i weep
blood
into my
butterfly
collection.
they used
to say
when
i was
a kid
i took
nothing
serious
but
in my
opinion
looking
back
was just
challenging
the false gods
who really
knew
nothing
at all about
this existence.

rough rider spitting up blood,

your only role-model...
the only angel on your shoulder
jake lamotta with a broken nose
going–*what's the matta, ya!*

doorman on strike again
in the upper east side...

transference,

with your insomnia you wake up
to the middle of *the twilight zone*
and this older contented bald man
in bed with his angelic wife in a
nightgown showing up to help him
out the door somewhere around dawn
to work the pig farm, get his dose of
methadone or practice the tightrope

you get up a little more motivated
with the world off your shoulders.

final call,

baby we should just finally move to vegas
to one of those magnificent classless schlock
imitation spanish haciendas with pillars
statues of david and elvis and mafioso
fountains and go out every so often no
betting problems and jerk the handles
and once a week do date night at the
*olive garden where when you're here
you're family* or whatever the hell
that spiel is and if don't get treated
like family something we both never
did experience anyway return back
to our mock mansion with marble
and mirrors all over the place
walls draped in wall to wall
velvet a sound-proof den
to keep *us against them*
and the other rooms filled
with out-of-work taxidermists,
hygienists, social workers,
soda jerks, senseis, petty
thieves, playboys, and
grown-up babysitters
join one of those book
of the month clubs or fruit
of the month clubs where we
can at least have something to
look forward to never look back on.

a postmodern version of cowboys & indians,

a.

just once i want to have an affair
with one of the visiting angels
who comes over once a week
to wrap my legs and our lips
will touch each other's due
to past abusive relationships
and be nothing passionate
but just cuz we both des
perately need it just once
i want to have an affair with
my primary this tall thin woman
with flat chest and a pale com
plexion who looks like she hasn't
gotten it in ages will be the prescription
the panacea for going through the motions
these rare moments usually the motivation
to get them out to see the neighborhood
the video stores the liquor the chinese

b.

the indian who lives in a thimble and blows his
long harmonica leaning against a wall drunker
looking over the williamette watching the logs

roll downriver from the lumbermill a warrant out
for him far from the res in montana staggering
over to the pooltable is his evening activity
is his freedom is his version of america

c.

the dope addicts who came all the way
from jersey manifest destiny on a grey
hound now scaling the outside pipes
of the whitewashed hotel on eddy
in the tenderloin district of frisco
their own personal slapstick version
of a comp room left out on the corner
eternally nodding-out in the dusk of
the mission and the fog of the pacific.

the dream,

last night i dreamed was rapping with kurt
cobaine and told him i thought he looked like
someone i knew called kurt cobaine. he seemed
to agree and had a very confused grin and
thought me funny reminding me of someone
i had always vibed with as a kid, but like
everything else, was ephemeral and ridiculous
for some strange reason ben affleck was also
in my dream and were hanging out on some fire
escape in the big city and really appeared to like
my sense of humor and were going back and
forth with keen observations, and for the rest
of the dream i was wearing some boy's neat
football uniform which i had always felt very
casual and comfortable in, and think it was
probably one of those good and positive
approval dreams because knew the next
day i was going to be interviewed by one
of these clinical ladies i already knew i knew
far more than and already knew all the answers
before she even knew the questions while most
likely would not offer me the position (which
i hoped she wouldn't) because deep-down
inside on a very shallow level somehow felt
intimidated and of course couldn't admit it.
when i woke up in the deep dark dawn and
walked over naked to the sink to get a drink

of water i thought i saw one of those old timers
like casey casum for like the *time-life* collection,
bawling out his co-host who stared very warmly
and endearingly into his eyes as though she was
hanging on his every word taking in his ad/vice
when i tried to get back to sleep that night
i wondered if death might not be like that
emotion of feeling guilty and wish/fantasy
never getting to that book always dreamed.

the last act at the all-you-can-eat dinner theater,

hey if i was to use this rusty razor
blade to cut right down the middle
of the spine of my arm would that
be my lifeline or deadline when
they always say they're gonna
reply or just the simple punch
line and why my whole life
have spent wearing masks
and dis guy is justice get
back at all obvious liars.
at my funeral all's i want
is that weird technicolor
audience with their insane
smiles some heckling some
howling that trapdoor where
they let in the banjo players
and fiddlers the slapstick
comedians the scholars
the sawdust floors where
ancient ancestors make
their early morning bagels
mix ice cream sodas and
heroin dunce in the corner
whispering sweet nothings
through the keyhole to the
sweet vagabond siren the
only one who can get through

to her the madmen and wanderers.
i was never one of those who ever
reached out for help or did one of
those infamous call-outs for help
but rather acted-out and couldn't
keep myself out of trouble and
turned to the hymns and mantras
of poets ritual call of rock & rollers.

like the hourglass figure of a miraculous
mermaid taking off to the horizon,

yur like a water
    fall wit
no more water
    to give
like bent over
    in prayer
wit just your
    sixth
sense & intuition
    herr spare
simple pretty poor
    trait
only thing left.

how to make caramel apples,

1. hope and pray
2. and hope and pray
3. and hope and pray
4. and hope and hope
5. and hope and pray
6. the apples come out this year
7. with all the mad mountain rain
8. melt down caramels in crockpot
9. have kids with black & blue marks & skinned knees stick popsicle sticks in and then watch them dance joyously to refrigerator
10. when they're done have them carefully take them out and take off wax paper
11. bite into them as if nothing else in the world matters and nothing means more
12. while nothing else does.

on bernard baruch,

    chewing that thin slice
              of bubblegum
                      from that pack
  of *topp's* baseball cards
        in my ripped soiled cords
                a sign of boyhood
                      courage
                action/adventure
        & having paid my dues
      hanging out
        with best pal
by that babbling brook
    behind the y
        dividing real life
            & my wild imagination
      some
        where
            in the mid-seventies
  seemed like a whole
other lifetime ago
      feeling instant guilt & remorse
              wash over me
                when dusk
    suddenly
showed up

        knowing i should be
                doing my homework
                        & not letting down my
parents
        i loved

bernard baruch's pop
            asked him what

                    he was going
            to do after he
    made his first million.

ralph & lenny,

i saw it all as a thoughtful boy
in my canvas pants with that
great big bandana patch and light
blue worn flannel floating deep
within those bottomless massive
leafpiles the sicilian gardeners
used to leave out on each
and every corner like sacred
pyramids wondering (or not
wondering at all) how they
got there becoming a part
of the lay of the land when
the chilly brooding dusk
was turning to mercurial
nightfall falling deep
into the spell of the
naturally warm lone
some leafy shelter
once again letting
my imagination run wild
and innocently worrying
about the future already
nihilistically contemplating
without being aware of it
about man's inhumanity
to man like some solitary
secret prayer with no
beginning and no end.

rap city in blue,

the firetrucks arrive on the pastel watercolor
scene helping c brown get his tangled kite
out of the tree after he gets blindsided
literally seeing stars when

lucy out of the clear blue sky obnoxiously yanks
that football from him just one more time and
him laid-out on the mound after getting knocked-
out with his clothes tossed all around

gingerly lifting him on the stretcher and
sympathetically asking if he's alright and
having gotten used to it becoming something
of a tradition routine & ritual inquiring how
are the wife and kids

back then with never an adult around in the
comic strip returning home from the hospital
all bandaged up a bit disoriented and seen
hitching on the side of the road

no opiates painkiller
just a long horizon
and a whole future
to look forward to.

bio-chem,

what the camera
should really focus
on and pan in on are
the pure beautiful legs
and bosoms of a cheer
leader who has every
one captivated under
her spell and influence
as opposed to the middle
aged coach having a sigh
got it meltdown and brow
beating the poor modest
long and lanky black
kid who processes
it as though he must
really care and give
a damn while a bunch
of loud and obnoxious
frat boys in the stands
pretend to make their
final stand feeling safe
and secure in their mob
mentality wielding their
wigger wannabe anatomies
and acting o so scary like
they're really something
you should worry about

as what it all really comes
down to in the long run
the final score are those
white girls with madonna
whore complexes who will
require a very stable provider
2-3 children a perfect pedigree
home in the suburbs and
the exclusive illusion of
living happily ever after.

mosaics or how not exactly to play dominos,

we fall in love with the image
before the thing before the person
women boogying at the roller disco…

    like dew dripping from the early morning gutter
        as fragile and solid as a blessed broken rocker

            picasso's portrait of old guitarist
            and pete townshend smashing it
            into a million pieces was culture

            allen ginsberg sticking his tongue
            through a hole he cut out in
            newspaper on the subway
            to try and get a reaction

            one of those yippies not sure which
            one; was it abbie hoffman or jerry
            rubin, tossing change over the
            balcony of the n.y. stock exchange
            watching them make a mad dash for it.

one of those bridges never quite finished
and knowing the spots not to step in,

when they give out those awards or i finally
    do one of those readings they'll discover me
bleeding, like one of those werewolves from
    the freak fangs of reality, never quite having
gotten closure in that 50's slick polyester
    espresso-brown businessman suit ripped
straight off the secondhand rack

the one i chose to nod-out in for special
    occasions when taking midnight buses
from lower manhattan to those strange
    vague shutdown postmodern squares
such as jersey city or patterson new
    jersey where all great journeys begin

to know all towns in america
    really began from the coalmines
deeply embedded in the plush verdant dewy hills
    at dawn and how i return or those revelations
with tears in my eyes looking out to sky
    lines irrelevant cause none of that matters

a whole pocket full of notes and
    observations and *hershey's kisses...*

ghetto,

man will fight quarrel cut throat and kill
for his own little plot of land whether it's
his postage stamp lawn in queens or king's
castle on the english countryside walt whitman
asking the operational question what is grass?
which is some pretty deep shit if you stop
to think about it as one day eventually
we'll all be six feet under say queens
more people buried below than over.

all-inclusive,

i guess the best
that can be expected
is they'll find me dead
after housekeeping just
turned down the covers
and those terrycloth
swans staring right
at each other at
the end of the bed
expedia having given
it a 4 star rating couple
empty extra postcards
on top the microwave
with a view of the
deep blue sea.

a different sort of sunblock,

i get all my news about
the destruction of the world
from one of those old russian
men with his shirt off letting
it all hang out on the warm and
wild summer boardwalk of brighton
beach, brooklyn with a little black
transistor planted on his shoulder
eternally stuck to his earlobe trying
his best to make out the message
through all the static and shriek of
seagulls literally lost in translation
while measuring his very measured
stoic and sentimental expressions
as often so hard to tell while such
a fine line between everyday sur-
vival and the end of the world.

Joseph Reich is a social worker who lives with his wife and fourteen year old son in the high-up mountains of Vermont. He has been published in a wide variety of eclectic literary journals both here and abroad, been nominated seven times for The Pushcart Prize, and his books in poetry and cultural studies include...

If I Told You To Jump Off The Brooklyn Bridge
(Flutter Press, 2009)

A Different Sort Of Distance
(Skive Magazine Press, 2010)

Pain Diary: Working Methadone & The Life & Times Of The Man Sawed In Half (Brick Road Poetry Press, 2010)

Drugstore Sushi (Thunderclap Press, 2010)

The Derivation Of Cowboys & Indians (Fomite Press, 2012)

The Housing Market: a comfortable place to jump off the end of the world (Fomite Press, 2013)

The Hole That Runs Through Utopia (Fomite Press, 2014)

Taking The Fifth And Running With It: a psychological guide for the hard of hearing and blind (Broadstone Books, 2015)

The Hospitality Business (Valeviel Press, 2015)

Connecting The Dots To Shangrila: A Postmodern Cultural Hx Of America (Fomite Press, 2016)

The Rituals Of Mummification (Sagging Meniscus Press, 2017)

American Existentialism (Tuba Press, 2017)

An Eccentric Urban Guide To Surviving (Analog Submission Press, 2017)

Magritte's Missing Murals: Insomniac Episodes (Sagging Meniscus Press, 2017)

How To Order Chinese During A Hostage Crisis: Dialects, Existential Essays, A Play, And Other Poems (Hog Press, 2017)

The American Book Of The Dead (Xi Draconis Books, 2018)

From Premonition To Prophecy (Delinkwent Scholar Press, 2018)

A Case Study of Werewolves (Fomite Press, 2018)

Statutes Of David (Pen & Anvil Press, 2018)

The Trouble With Authority (Makeshift Press, 2019)

www.ingramcontent.com/pod-product-compliance
Lightning Source LLC
Chambersburg PA
CBHW030322100526
44592CB00010B/527